The Art of The
PERFECT
DEFENSE

RONALD D. HEDDING, ESQ.

The Art of the
PERFECT
DEFENSE

**Your Essential Guide
To Criminal Defense
In Los Angeles**

RONALD D. HEDDING, ESQ.

This book is dedicated to my four amazing children,
who inspire and make me proud every day:
Shane, Mary, Lily, and Violet

ACKNOWLEDGMENTS

I'd like to thank my parents, Ron and Sylvia. From the baseball diamond to the LA County courtroom, they taught me to perform under pressure and encouraged me to do my best in everything I pursue.

And special thanks to Lawrence Ineno for your continued support and insight.

TABLE OF CONTENTS

Introduction

As a kid growing up in Los Angeles, I loved being able to play outdoor sports year round. Later, when I became a dad, I sought to instill the same values of competitiveness, responsibility, teamwork, and fairness into my children's lives.

Over the past decade, I've coached nearly forty youth sports teams. Becoming a coach allowed me to connect with my kids in a way we'll all cherish for the rest of our lives. I know this because some of my fondest childhood memories involve my parents' hands-on approach to my athletic development.

On the one hand, criminal defense law seems completely unrelated to baseball and soccer—my favorite sports to coach. On the other, so many of the skills required to be a top athlete are similar to those of running a respected law firm. Being a successful local business owner and community member means I must be a team player and follow the rules; being an advocate on my clients' behalf requires me to love winning and despise defeat; and skillfully representing my clients in court involves performing under pressure with calm, confidence, and competence.

Throughout my career, I have constantly found ways to apply the lessons sports taught me into my law practice. By always striving to win, working harder than the competition, gaining higher-quality skills, and having more skin in the game, I would earn the respect of judges, prosecutors, and my colleagues. The end result would be to represent my clients better than anyone else.

The book you're reading highlights everything I've learned, experienced, and accomplished within LA's criminal justice system. You'll be gaining unparalleled insight into finding the best lawyer to protect and serve your interests and ways to navigate our county's complex court system. You'll also learn how to avoid pitfalls that could ruin your life, the lives of those you care about, or both.

You won't find another criminal defense book that is as comprehensive, user-friendly, and focused on Los Angeles. "Why just LA when our criminal defense system is nationwide?" you may ask. Because our county covers one of the most highly populated regions in the United States, being a specialist in the area, knowing its local laws, and skillfully navigating LA's nuances are essential to experiencing the best possible outcome. The devil *is* in the details, and *The Art of the Perfect Defense* covers key information to help keep you out of the inferno. This book will play an important role in your overall criminal defense strategy. Here's to getting you back on track.

A FINAL NOTE: Throughout this book, I'll point to differences between private criminal defense lawyers and public defenders. There are excellent public defenders, and there are mediocre ones—just as there are excellent private attorneys and average ones.

In my opinion, hiring a criminal defense attorney is the best choice a person can make when being charged with a crime because a skilled lawyer has the advantage of time and preparation. Of course, finding the right lawyer is the key. This book is meant to educate you on a system and an attorney's role in that system. At the same time, my hope is this book will help you make the right choices that lead to the most favorable outcome for you and those you care about.

CHAPTER 1
Setting Yourself Up for Success

Consider the following possibilities:

- You've been bailed or have been cited out or released from custody with a court date that's approximately thirty days away. You have a criminal case pending against you.

- Your son or daughter, nephew or niece, grandchild, friend, or employee has been taken into custody.

- You've discovered that you or someone you care about is the target of a criminal investigation.

Does any one of the above scenarios apply to you? If so, I wrote this book for you. When your freedom and reputation, or that of those close to you, are on the line, developing a solid defense and strategy to deal with the case is your most important objective. In this chapter, you'll learn the three-part formula to experiencing the best possible outcome and protecting your rights.

Band-Aids over Bullet Wounds

I've spent twenty-five years preparing and representing defendants in Los Angeles County's criminal court system. Throughout my career, I've seen every criminal scenario imaginable in a metropolis as vast and diverse as ours: violent crimes, drugs, sex offenses, DUIs, hit and runs, thefts, juvenile crimes, weapons charges, and more. Despite seeing people on both sides of the law at their worst, I'm a firm believer that no matter what, you can find good in every person and situation.

My optimistic outlook may seem far-fetched and perhaps insensitive to your plight and the tough times you're facing—without a doubt, being charged or placed in custody or both is one of the scariest events you could ever encounter. But, time and time again, I've witnessed remarkable strength and courage from clients who are confronting life-altering circumstances. As the saying goes, "It is during our darkest moments that we must focus to see the light."

When you're in the early stages of dealing with law enforcement, your fears and anxieties may be reaching their peak. But making hasty decisions without considering possible after-effects is like putting a Band-Aid over a bullet wound: You may be temporarily addressing the problem right now, but in the end, your efforts won't provide any long-term relief.

Three-part Formula for Peace of Mind

Imagine that Monica received an urgent call from her son, Daniel. He has just been arrested and is pleading with his mom to post bail.

"You and Dad have gotta get me outa here!" Daniel says.

Monica's parenting is put to the test: Daniel is distressed and behaving irrationally, and she's terrified about her son's future. On the one hand, she wants to help him out. On the other, her family's financial funds are limited.

To help their son, Monica and her husband empty their savings from their bank accounts. The couple then post bail. Once Daniel's back at home, he and his parents plan to reach out to attorneys. Unfortunately, they've now run out of money to hire one.

The three-part formula to making good decisions during turbulent times is as follows:

7

1. Identify what you can control

2. Maintain objectivity

3. Hire a top criminal defense attorney *as soon as possible*

First, when you're the target of a criminal investigation, identifying what you can control will empower you when you feel completely powerless. No doubt you'll be confronted with countless what-if scenarios: What if I'm convicted? What if I go to jail? What if I go broke? What if my life is ruined?

But rather than dwell on questions with no firm answer, your energy will be better spent focusing on what is within your control. Just as in life, in criminal defense, knowledge is power. By spending time educating yourself, you'll identify how you can best protect your interests or those of someone you care about.

Second, when faced with one of the biggest obstacles you'll ever encounter, maintaining objectivity is key to making wise decisions that will provide the most favorable result.

For example, what if Daniel and his parents had taken a moment to rationally consider their options, rather than succumbed to their frenzied state? They might have realized that hiring an attorney first would have been the best use of their limited resources.

Once on the case, a reputable criminal defense lawyer could have used his expertise to lower the bail, have Daniel released on his own recognizance (in other words, requiring no payment), or questioned the benefit of posting bail if jail time was inevitable.

In my experience, I've met countless clients who later regretted posting bail because they hadn't considered the multiple consequences of doing so—consequences you'll read about in subsequent chapters.

Third, Daniel's example is one of many that points to the importance of working with a skilled lawyer as soon as possible. A strong lawyer who focuses on criminal defense in Los Angeles will leverage his or her local expertise and act aggressively on your behalf. Your attorney will tap into his or her years of experience to navigate through Los Angeles's enormous criminal justice system. He or she will be your source for guidance, support, and peace of mind.

Identifying what you can control and maintaining objectivity are challenging, if not downright impossible, when faced with the force of one of the nation's most powerful institutions. Hiring a top criminal defense attorney as soon as possible is your gateway to taking back control of your predicament and introducing objectivity.

In a seemingly endless sea of attorneys to choose from, finding a strong lawyer is difficult. Unfortunately, the consequences of working with a mediocre or incompetent attorney could quite literally put your freedom at risk. The good news is you'll dramatically improve the outcome of your search when you invest time researching and educating yourself.

In the next chapters, I'll help you identify aspects of your case that you can control and provide an objective perspective when your outlook is clouded by confusion, fear, and uncertainty. You'll also learn strategies to find the best lawyer to meet your needs. In the next chapter, I'll break down Los Angeles County's complex criminal justice system so you'll gain a basic understanding of how it works. You'll also learn the key terms that will apply to your case.

CHAPTER 2
Don't Bury Your Head in the Sand

Ben was arrested on a domestic violence charge in Van Nuys. It was Friday, and the police officer informed him a public defender couldn't meet him until Monday, which meant unless he posted his fifty-thousand-dollar bail, he'd be in jail for four days.

His first instinct was to phone his girlfriend, which would be a mistake considering she had called 911 in the first place. And as much as he wanted to reach out to his family, they would be furious once he confessed what had happened.

Being one person in a system designed to deal with tens of thousands of defendants left Ben feeling powerless, vulnerable, and scared. Meanwhile, he was stuck in a cramped jail cell and couldn't wait to get out, and he had no idea how to navigate the complexities of LA's massive criminal justice system.

Ben wondered if he should hire a lawyer—but he had no idea where to start his search. He considered bailing out—but he wasn't sure if it would be a wise move to use his limited resources to pay for it. He wondered if he would receive fair treatment within a reasonable amount of time or become lost within an unwieldy bureaucracy.

In this chapter, we'll explore Ben's predicament. Through his experience, you'll gain essential insight as you determine the best course of action for your particular case.

BEN'S FIRST OPTION
Working with a Public Defender

Uncertain how to proceed and with limited resources, Ben decides *not* to post bail. As much as he dreads thinking about it, his decision means he'll remain in custody over the weekend. He spends the next three days locked up, sleeping on a cold, dirty cement floor, and surrounded by inmates who could benefit from a hot shower and strong soap.

At 5:00 a.m. on Monday morning, he's abruptly woken up by the flurry of activity around him. He and his fellow inmates are directed out of their cell.

"Keep moving," a law enforcement officer repeatedly shouts to the group of men.

They are corralled onto a bus.

"Where are they taking us?" he asks the man next to him.

"The IRC," the stranger responds.

The Inmate Reception Center (IRC), located at 450 Bauchet Street in downtown Los Angeles, is the county's main male inmate intake and release facility. The massive complex can hold nineteen thousand men, and it handles all bookings, housing classifications, and medical screenings and treatments for individuals entering LA's jail system. In addition, the IRC maintains and stores all inmate records, clothing, property, and funds. It is also the primary inmate transfer point to the state prison system, the immigration and customs enforcement, and other government agencies.

Although Ben is in Van Nuys, he and his fellow inmates will be bused across the city to the IRC in downtown LA. After they're processed there, they'll then be returned to the Valley the same day to appear in court.

At 11:00 a.m., Ben arrives back in Van Nuys. Two hours later, he meets with Carlos, his public defender. Carlos is hardworking and overwhelmed with a caseload that expands with every round of state budget cuts. When he sits down with Ben in the back courtroom lock-up, Carlos has a stack of files in his hands. Ben is clearly one among many cases Carlos must address today. The lawyer briefly thumbs through Ben's file, which marks the first time he's reviewed his client's case.

"What happened isn't my fault," Ben says. He then explains his version of events.

"Okay," says Carlos. "I recommend you enter a not guilty **plea,** but the decision is completely up to you."

What is a plea?

This is when you formally tell the judge your answer to the criminal complaint. You'll learn more about this in this chapter's arraignment section.

This is Ben's first arrest. With no legal background from which to make a well-informed decision, Ben believes it's in his best interest to follow Carlos's suggestion. At the same time, he questions Carlos's recommendation because it was based on a quick review of his file and the limited time he had to hear Ben's side of the story.

"Do you have any questions?" Carlos asks.

Ben doesn't even know where to start: What's a plea? What are my options? What are the pros and cons of any decision I make? I've never appeared before a judge before, so what do I say?

Ben begins with the following:

What's going to happen next?

The question is loaded. In other words, in order to receive a complete and detailed answer, Carlos will need time to listen to Ben's account. Unfortunately, Carlos has many other inmates to see. Thus, at this juncture, the public defender doesn't have time to have a meaningful discussion with Ben regarding the case.

Carlos leaves to speak with the next inmate. The brief meeting leaves Ben feeling lost and frustrated.

"What if my story is completely different from the police report?" Ben thinks to himself.

A law enforcement officer then directs Ben to a holding tank within the courtroom, and he waits for his **arraignment**.

What is an arraignment?

This is an initial court appearance where a defendant is brought before a judge to answer a criminal charge or charges. Arraignments do not address a defendant's perspective regarding the charges. In other words, defendants won't be asked about their version of events.

During an arraignment, the defendant may enter a plea. Options include guilty, not guilty, no contest, continue the arraignment, or set the case for the Early Disposition Program (EDP), which allows those charged with a felony to attempt to have their cases resolved early. A chance of receiving a more favorable plea bargain is one of the benefits of the EDP.

At 4:00 p.m., the judge calls Ben's case, and Carlos joins Ben in the courtroom.

"Do you understand you have the right to a speedy trial?" the judge asks Ben.

"Yes, Your Honor," says Ben.

In reality, Ben has no idea what he just agreed to.

"Counsel, what's your pleasure?" the judge asks Carlos.

"My client is entering a not guilty plea," Carlos says.

The judge then sets the date for a preliminary hearing, which will determine if there is "reasonable suspicion" Ben is guilty of the charge(s). During the **preliminary hearing**, witnesses will be called and evidence presented. At the end, the judge will determine whether sufficient evidence exists to bind Ben over for trial. (Bind is a legal term that basically means hold a person.)

Not Guilty Pleas, Preliminary Hearings, and EDPs

In general, entering a not guilty plea is assuming an *offensive position*. Thus, once you take this stance, you're signaling the prosecution to develop the strongest case possible to challenge your plea. As a result, when the time comes for your preliminary hearing, you should expect the prosecution to have pooled its resources, which includes lining up witnesses and preparing the prosecution's case against you.

The EDP, on the other hand, signals you seek to resolve the case through negotiations if possible. If the EDP doesn't provide the outcome you seek, you can still set the case for preliminary hearing and challenge the prosecution's case. But if a preliminary hearing is set first, *you lose the EDP option.*

Both a not guilty plea and an EDP may have their place in a person's defense—there's no one-size-fits-all option. But making the right decision requires experience, research, and developing a customized strategy particular to your case.

Ben's hearing is scheduled for ten days away and will be located in a different courtroom. Because public defenders are typically assigned to work in a particular courtroom, *Ben will have a new public defender during his next hearing.* For example, the Van Nuys court has multiple courtrooms in the same courthouse. It has one arraignment courtroom for felonies and one for misdemeanors and multiple courtrooms for preliminary hearings. EDPs and arraignments take place in the same courtroom. Courtroom dynamics throughout LA County vary from courthouse to courthouse.

"**Bail** is set at fifty thousand dollars," the judge says. In this scenario, the public defender might have argued for Ben to be released on his own recognizance. His argument might or might not have been successful. This is an important aspect of the plea because it may determine whether Ben remains in custody another ten days.

How is bail determined?

Judges typically set bail during an arraignment. The judge uses a bail schedule, which is a guideline that assigns a dollar amount to a particular crime. Thus the bail amount is usually based on a formula. For a given crime, felony bail is higher than misdemeanor bail. In fact, for a misdemeanor, bail is usually not necessary.

Once bail is set in a case, it usually isn't lowered or raised, unless there are "changed circumstances." For instance, if a lawyer convinces a judge to lower a crime from a felony to a misdemeanor, this would constitute changed circumstances and possibly warrant a bail reduction.

Ben buried his head in the sand—and now he'll potentially have to pay the price in more ways than one.

Ben didn't phone his family, he remained in custody, and—depending on whether his bail was reduced—he might stay locked up until the preliminary hearing.

He has lost control. If he has to bail out, it will be expensive and he potentially has missed the opportunity to negotiate his case in the most favorable setting possible—the EDP court. As you'll read in the next section, by doing nothing, Ben gained nothing. Neglecting to hire an attorney—one who would have the time to thoroughly prepare before meeting Ben—turned out to be financially and emotionally costly.

In the meantime, because Ben's case is set for a preliminary hearing, the prosecution will be working hard to prove its case. Ben has taken an offensive position, and the prosecution will respond in kind. The prosecution will do everything in its power to make sure his girlfriend will testify against him. And she will most likely be frustrated, if not downright angry, that she is being forced to appear in court for an act committed against her. The prosecution will also be certain the police officers will show up to testify against Ben.

BEN'S SECOND OPTION
Hiring a Private Criminal Defense Lawyer

In this scenario, rather than wait to meet the public defender, Ben takes a different approach: Stuck in a cell and filled with anxiety, Ben decides to call his family for help. He knows once he makes the call, he'll never hear the end of it: You're *where?!* You *really* messed up this time. How are we going to pay for a lawyer?

But the thought of remaining in a dirty, smelly cell for the next four days, the feeling of helplessness, and not knowing what will happen next are too much for him to bear. So he gets a phone call out to his parents seeking their help. After receiving a verbal lashing over the phone, Ben pleads with his dad to intervene.

Once they complete their phone conversation, Ben's mom and dad consider their options. With their limited budget, they can either bail him out or retain a lawyer—but they can't afford to do both.

Because his parents aren't under the pressure of being in custody, they are able to think through their options more objectively than their incarcerated son can. As a result, they realize if they bail him out, they'll be left with no money to hire a lawyer. No doubt they want their son out of jail, but they also believe the best long-term solution may not provide Ben the immediate release he seeks. Despite Ben's demands, his parents forego bail and direct their resources to hiring a highly skilled Los Angeles criminal defense attorney.

Ben's parents decide to hire Julie, who is a top Los Angeles criminal defense lawyer.

For twenty years, Julie has successfully defended countless domestic violence charges. She also frequently appears in the Van Nuys criminal court.

Right away, Julie interviews Ben's parents to gain as much intelligence about Ben as possible—information that will help her develop the best strategy to resolve his case and potentially assist in Ben's release. She asks them the following questions:

1. **What's Ben's relationship with the woman he's accused of battering?**

    This question requires asking the following sub-questions: Are they a married or an unmarried couple, do they have kids in common, or did they just meet? Is there a divorce in process?

This information could be helpful at a potential bail hearing, negotiation, or even a trial.

2. How does this woman feel about Ben now?

For instance, she may regret what happened, or she may be out for blood. If the woman is regretful, Julie can potentially assist Ben to reach a fair resolution. But if she's out for blood, the woman will be angry and eager to help punish Ben. The woman's attitude will likely influence the prosecutor and the case he or she creates against Ben.

3. What are Ben's character and personality like?

This involves identifying his role in the community, employment status, and any children who rely on him financially and emotionally. The judge will want to know this information at a bail hearing. Thus, Julie will most likely use these facts to negotiate or litigate on Ben's behalf.

4. What is Ben's employment status?

This question addresses whether Ben is the family's sole breadwinner or not. In addition, being in custody may result in Ben losing his job, which will make a difficult situation even worse.

5. **If Ben has any children, what are their ages?**

    If his kids are all young and he is a main caregiver, being in custody may adversely impact the family unit.

6. **Does his family live close?**

    This issue relates to **flight risk**, in other words, the likelihood Ben will leave the county, state, or country and not make his court appearance. For instance, if his family lives in Los Angeles, California, this *decreases* his flight risk. But if his family lives in Lima, Peru, this *increases* his flight risk.

7. **Is he a US citizen? If not, how long has he been here?**

    This is another flight-risk-related question. At the time of setting bail, if Ben isn't a US citizen, the judge may be concerned Ben will leave the country.

8. **Did the family speak to him before or after the crime in question took place? If so, what did they discuss?**

    No doubt, Ben has his version of what happened and why. Maybe some information can be gathered, investigated, or both *before* the arraignment so Julie will be ready to argue and negotiate from multiple angles.

9. **Has Ben been involved in behavior like this before?**
   If no, the judge may consider Ben's poor judgment an aberration and give him the benefit of the doubt when deciding whether to release him. If yes, Julie will need to know because the prosecutor will certainly bring this up.

The answers to these questions will allow Julie to begin preparing a customized defense for her client. For example, based on what she discovers, she may realize he has a high likelihood of being released on his **own recognizance**.

What does own recognizance mean?

When a defendant is granted an own recognizance (OR) release, he won't be required to pay any bail money. In exchange for release, the defendant pledges to show up to all future court proceedings. When deciding to grant an OR release, a judge asks himself or herself the following:

- How serious is the crime?
- What is the defendant's criminal record?
- Is the defendant a danger to the community?
- Is the defendant a flight risk?
- Has the defendant ever failed to appear in court before?

Julie arranges to arrive at the Van Nuys courthouse on Monday armed with the information provided by Ben's parents. Ben's case is the only one on her calendar for the day, which means she can give her client undivided attention that will provide him with peace of mind during these uncertain times. By circumstance, this is an advantage Julie has over the public defender. It isn't the public defender's fault he or she doesn't have the time necessary to fully research a defendant's case right away; rather, the way the system is set up results in this scenario.

After entering the Van Nuys courthouse, Julie promptly reviews the police report. She then meets with the prosecutor. During their discussion, she hears the prosecutor's perspective regarding the charges. Understanding the opposing side's arguments is an important step she always takes to determine her options. As she gathers more and more information, she uses it to decide the strategy her client should employ.

At 11:00 a.m., Ben returns from the IRC, and Julie meets with him. During their talk, she listens to Ben's account of what took place prior to his arrest, which gives her a necessary piece of the investigative puzzle. She then has a fact-intensive discussion with Ben where she compares his account with the police report. Based on her conversation with the prosecutor and her review of the police report, she tells Ben what she believes the prosecutor will argue in front of the judge.

"Your crime will be taken seriously, but your actions of pushing your girlfriend aren't the worst I've seen. You have no prior criminal record, you're a low risk to flee the jurisdiction, you've got a good job, you're supporting your three-year-old child, and you're a low risk to reoffend against your girlfriend," she says.

"How do you know all this?" Ben asks.

"I have already spoken to your parents and performed preliminary research. I'm prepared and confident we'll get you out on your own recognizance. That way you'll avoid having to post a **bond**. Once you're out, we'll sit down in my office after you've read the police report and decide our next steps. For now, I'll continue the arraignment so we don't miss any opportunities to negotiate if that's what we decide to do," she says.

What is a bond?

If the judge followed the bail schedule and set Ben's bail at fifty thousand dollars and Ben can't afford to bail out, he has the option of hiring a certified bail bondsman to cover his bail. The bondsman charges a percentage of the bail amount in exchange for assuming the risk Ben may **jump bail**—in other words, if Ben doesn't show up to his court date. The bond is typically 10 percent of the bail amount and often requires collateral too. So in Ben's case, the bondsman would charge him five thousand dollars. Ben won't receive this money back.

Julie then explains her strategy and their options:

1. She'll address bail first. If the judge agrees to an own recognizance release, she will not set the case for the preliminary hearing. Instead, she'll continue the arraignment in the EDP court for thirty days away, which will give her the time she needs to thoroughly investigate the case. (On the other hand, if Ben will remain in custody, typically defense attorneys schedule their hearings for as few days as possible after the initial arraignment because they don't want their clients to needlessly languish in jail.)

2. If Ben is released on his own recognizance and they decide to request a preliminary hearing, they will have thirty days to develop their defense.

She then provides a step-by-step description of the arraignment proceedings, she explains courtroom etiquette and what he should do and why, and she gives detailed and easy-to-understand answers to all his questions.

By the end of their meeting, Julie has organized a strong case for her client. Because private criminal defense attorneys typically receive priority to have their cases called first, Ben's case is handled right after the court's lunch recess.

"Counsel, what's your pleasure?" the judge asks Julie.

"Your Honor, before we set any dates, we'd like to be heard on bail," Julie confidently says.

Julie then accurately describes Ben's positive attributes. Her appeal for Ben's OR release is based on the information she gleaned from her interview with Ben and his parents. She effectively convinces the judge, who releases Ben on his own recognizance.

Ben is relieved he'll be freed after the hearing. Julie knows this has alleviated a tremendous amount of pressure from her client, which will allow him to focus on his defense. Julie then requests to continue the arraignment and set the matter for the EDP court. If granted, this means Ben's case will remain in the Van Nuys arraignment courtroom, which also handles EDPs.

"You understand you have the right to a speedy trial and preliminary hearing. Do you waive these rights in order to continue the arraignment?" the judge asks Ben.

"Yes, Your Honor," says Ben.

The judge sets the next hearing thirty days later. Ben is reunited with his family that day. Because he was released on his own recognizance, his family was spared the expense of posting a five-thousand-dollar bond.

A Review of the Two Options

Option 1: By entering a not guilty plea and pushing for a preliminary hearing, Ben remained in custody, possibly for another ten days. As he suffered in his cell, the prosecution was forming the strongest case possible against him in order to undermine his not guilty plea. Taking an offensive position was a declaration of war on Ben's part. In addition, because he agreed to a preliminary hearing, he forfeited the opportunity to participate in the EDP.

Option 2: Because Julie was properly prepared, Ben was released on his own recognizance. For the next thirty days, he and his attorney will focus on developing the strongest defense possible. In the event the EDP doesn't provide the outcome they seek, he has the option to schedule a preliminary hearing later on.

In the event the EDP works to his advantage, he'll receive a more favorable plea bargain than would otherwise be the case.

To Julie, every case and every client is different, which means she never employs a one-size-fits-all strategy when it comes to protecting her clients' rights, reputations, career, and freedom. She prides herself on the favorable results her clients experience and her track record of success.

Through Ben's experience, I've provided a broad overview of the steps defendants go through when they are charged with a crime. Next, I'll introduce you to the basics of Los Angeles County's complex criminal defense system.

CHAPTER 3
An Overview of
Los Angeles Criminal Courts

LA County's court system is one of the largest unified trial systems in the world. It comprises around 40 courthouses that include nearly 600 courtrooms and 450 judges. The system handles 2.7 million cases and 5,500 jury trials each year. During the pendency of a case, defense attorneys are dealing with judges; prosecutors, including city or district attorneys; bailiffs; court reporters and clerks; and other government employees who make up the system's nearly 4,500-person workforce.

In today's times of underfunded and overburdened state courts, services have been dramatically cut, which makes protecting your best interests more difficult than ever. For instance, given their ever-expanding caseloads and shoestring budgets, prosecutors and their staff have little patience for those who are ill-equipped to navigate the big court system.

No doubt, dealing with such a vast, complicated, and gigantic organization is overwhelming, particularly if you aren't familiar with its complexity. Unfortunately, overlooking even the smallest detail regarding your case could compromise your freedom.

In this chapter, you'll learn who the most important individuals in your case will be. I'll also provide essential information about our county's criminal justice system. This information will form the foundation of your plan to develop the perfect defense for your particular situation.

Criminal Justice System versus Civil Arena

When you hear someone say, "There are too many lawyers!" the complaint typically refers to the **civil arena**, which largely focuses on resolving disputes over money. Examples of civil-arena cases include lawsuits over wills, trusts, and contracts. In addition, the civil arena comprises family law, which is commonly called divorce court. The reality is the civil arena has an overabundance of attorneys.

Meanwhile, the **criminal justice system** focuses on one's freedom stemming from charges related to felonies;

DUIs; domestic violence; three-strikes cases; sex, theft, drug, and juvenile crimes; and more.

Despite the fact that LA's criminal system covers one of the country's biggest cities, when it comes to great criminal defense attorneys, Los Angeles County's criminal justice community is small, and the group of the best lawyers is even smaller—in general, veteran criminal defense attorneys, prosecutors, and judges all know each other.

Top attorneys have worked with all the key players who will influence your case's outcome. They understand an individual judge's *judicial temperament*. This refers to a judge's overall approach to the law, prosecutors, defense attorneys, and defendants. It also describes a judge's compassion, decisiveness, open-mindedness, courtesy, patience, freedom from bias, and commitment to equal justice for all under the law.

LA's best attorneys are familiar with the prosecutors in each court in addition to bailiffs. Furthermore, they know how to communicate effectively with court staff, and they realize the importance of knowing all the players in the criminal court system.

In my experience, the criminal court system upholds a higher degree of ethics and fairness as compared to the civil arena. For instance, you see much more bureaucracy and red tape in the civil court system. And attorneys in the civil arena have an inherent conflict of interest when they *bill per hour*—the longer their clients duke out a case, the more their attorneys can bill for time. Meanwhile, criminal defense attorneys frequently *bill by flat fee*. Thus criminal defense attorneys are rewarded for efficiently resolving the case, whether that means trying it before a jury or negotiating aggressively on a defendant's behalf.

As far as the courthouses themselves are concerned, criminal courts and civil courts are separate in Los Angeles. For instance, in Van Nuys, you have Van Nuys East, which handles civil cases, and you have Van Nuys West, which is the criminal courthouse. Federal cases are an exception. In the federal system, federal judges handle both criminal and civil matters. Overall, you'll find more criminal courthouses than civil ones. And criminal trials typically take precedence between the two.

Federal versus State Crimes

Broadly speaking, the difference between **federal** and **state crimes** is that federal defendants and their crimes are more sophisticated than their state counterparts. As a result, the charges and punishments associated with federal crimes are typically more severe.

In general, crimes include the following three types:

1. **Felonies**—high-grade crimes involving serious harm.

2. **Misdemeanors**—low-grade crimes that typically don't involve serious harm.

3. **Infractions**—public offenses, such as traffic violations and other low-grade issues.

What are sophisticated crimes?

They are complex crimes that cause more harm to the public, require planning, leverage trust, or all three. For example, when an employee embezzles funds from his employer, this crime is more sophisticated than a customer shoplifting from a store. This is because the employee is in a position of trust. The more sophisticated the crime, the harsher the penalty will be.

You'll find overlap between felonies and misdemeanors. For example, a DUI is often a misdemeanor. But if someone is injured, it may be elevated to a felony. Similarly, domestic violence is typically a misdemeanor, unless serious injury is involved or there are prior convictions for the offender, in which case it will be charged as a felony.

The Cast of Characters

The following are the men and women who will influence, organize, and make decisions related to your case.

Law enforcement is responsible for investigating and arresting those involved in criminal behavior. Law enforcement includes sheriffs, the Los Angeles Police Department, the FBI, the Secret Service, and the Department of Homeland Security.

Prosecutors are attorneys who work on behalf of citizens. Prosecutors control the charges filed against a criminal defendant. They prosecute cases for the county and state. Prosecutors include the following:

- **District attorneys** (DAs) work for the people of the state of California and typically prosecute felonies.

- **City attorneys** work for the city of Los Angeles and typically prosecute misdemeanors.

Judges preside over criminal cases, felonies, misdemeanors, and infractions. They control the sentence meted out to the criminal defendant. Judges exert the most power when it comes to sentencing, and prosecutors exert the most power when it comes to charges. Their roles are like the executive and legislative branches of government: The president is more effective with foreign affairs, compared to Congress, which is more effective with domestic ones.

Bailiffs are law enforcement officers who are in the courtroom. They preserve order, and they deal with the defendants who are in custody.

Court reporters record everything said in courts while the judge is on the record. Court reporters also provide records of court proceedings.

Court clerks run the paperwork, the calendar, and the court procedurally and deal with motions. Court clerks also facilitate communication between judges and lawyers. Think of them as the middle people the lawyers directly deal with.

Juror is someone who listens to courtroom jury trials. Jurors are members of the community enlisted as volunteers in order to hear both criminal and civil cases. Under the "One-Day or One-Trial Jury Service," Californians are required to serve in jury trials once every twelve months. According to the Administrative Office of the Courts, those called to serve can fulfill their requirement through one of four ways:

1. Be assigned to on-call or standby jury service.

2. Appear in person for jury service.

3. Appear in person for jury service or be assigned to a courtroom for jury selection but not chosen for a trial.

4. Appear in person for jury service, be assigned to a courtroom for jury selection, and be chosen for a trial.

Criminal Defense Attorneys defend those who are charged with crimes and protect their constitutional rights, reputation, and freedom.

Setting

Courthouse—A building typically located in the heart of a city's downtown area, the courthouse has jurisdiction over all the crimes committed in a designated boundary. The location where a crime is committed determines which courthouse has jurisdiction over that crime. In Los Angeles County, each of the estimated forty courthouses has an area of land within its jurisdiction. This number has fluctuated due to budget constraints and court closures.

In general, highly sophisticated, political, or heinous federal crimes committed in LA County are adjudicated in the following two downtown Los Angeles federal courthouses:

- The Roybal Federal Building located at
  255 East Temple Street, Los Angeles 90012

- United States Courthouse located at
  312 North Spring Street, Los Angeles 90012

Knowing the Basics Will Set You Up for Success

When you're fighting for your freedom, sometimes "the best defense is a strong offense." While other times, negotiation is the only reasonable choice. Deciding upon an option is difficult, particularly when you're scared and confused. Here is where understanding the basics of the system—one whose outcomes may affect the rest of your life, as well as the lives of those you care about—will bring clarity to your perspective. By combining your efforts with the expertise of a seasoned and savvy defense attorney, you're ensuring that you'll experience the best possible result.

Now that you've received an overview of the criminal court system, you're ready for the following step. In the next chapter, you'll learn about Los Angeles criminal defense lawyers.

CHAPTER 4
Is Your Lawyer Battle Tested or Trial-and-Error?

Lisa recently graduated from law school and passed the State Bar of California, which qualifies her to practice law in Los Angeles. She is one of around forty-five thousand freshly minted law school graduates who become lawyers every year. These individuals are highly educated—and mostly unemployed. Saddled with a one-hundred-thousand-dollar student loan, Lisa is hungry for work.

"You gotta spend money to make it," she reminds herself. Lisa hires an expensive marketing company to design her fancy website. She pays big bucks for top placement within online searches. As a result, when prospects look for lawyers on their smartphones and computers, her name appears high in search results.

Lisa's site promotes her as a "Top Los Angeles Criminal Defense Attorney." It also says that Lisa practices criminal defense and can do everything better than her competitors. But what her prospects don't know is she lacks any real-world courtroom experience defending clients. The truth is she's an all-around rookie with no battle-tested experience.

When it comes to protecting your freedom and rights, how do you avoid hiring an attorney that doesn't have the experience and skill to be your strongest ally? In this chapter, you'll learn about the three broad categories of criminal defense lawyers currently practicing in Los Angeles County. From this information, you can determine the type of lawyer that will best meet your needs.

Low Skill: Style over Substance

One of Lisa's highest priorities is to gain experience. "Just a few high-profile cases under my belt, and I'll be set," she reminds herself.

Unfortunately, whoever hires her will be placing his or her future in the hands of an unseasoned amateur—an inexperienced attorney without the deep knowledge of how to maneuver successfully within Los Angeles's complex criminal justice system.

If Lisa were a new scientist, then her prospective clients would be nothing more than experimental lab rats. She would be applying untested strategies on them and conducting trial-and-error experiments—all in hopes to build her résumé.

One of the main pitfalls of this approach when working with people in the court system, rather than rats in a lab, is prospective clients have no assurance the outcome of their cases will not end in disaster.

In the next chapter, you'll learn how to spot the strength of battle-tested attorneys. This will allow you to separate the veterans from the newcomers. For now, know that high placement in search engines and slick websites are no guarantee that the lawyer is a superb master of his or her craft. While many top lawyers have content-rich sites, you must look beyond what you discover online.

Next, we'll explore the second level of attorney.

Middle Skill: The Mill Practice

Adam works for a successful law firm that handles hundreds of cases a year. His boss, Rebecca, was one of LA's most successful criminal defense lawyers. But that was over twenty years ago. Since then, Rebecca has entered semi-retirement. While she has maintained her status as firm figurehead, she rarely practices law. In fact, she spends most of her time at her Malibu beachfront home, and she hardly ever shows up at her Beverly Hills office.

In her place, Rebecca has hired a team of attorneys. Her team practices under the power of her personal brand—one that for years has appeared on billboards, buses, TV commercials, and at the top of Google search results. Like Rebecca, many attorneys with solid reputations who advertise on the Internet no longer practice criminal defense.

If law firms throughout Los Angeles were restaurants, then mill attorneys, such as those on Rebecca's team, would be on par with chain establishments.

When defendants hire mill attorneys, they're most likely paying the firm's founder and figurehead, whose image appears on all of its high-profile marketing. But the famous face of the rainmaker will *never* show up in court to defend his or her clients. Attorneys working within a mill practice sacrifice autonomy and control over their own professional destiny in exchange for the safety of a steady paycheck that comes from their well-known boss.

In addition, the firm's figurehead compensates mill attorneys such as Adam. Which means that no matter how much time Adam puts into a particular case, his pay is the same. This type of arrangement creates distance between Adam and his clients. Thus he'll inherently have less interest in their cases. Adam will also have little incentive to invest the extra hours that may make the difference between his client's freedom and an unfavorable outcome. Lastly, while Adam may have great intuition and judgment, his compensation doesn't reward him for applying his highest level of expertise to his clients' cases.

Within the past five years, the mill model has become more common. Business people have leveraged their corporate savvy to create profitable large-scale criminal defense firms. One of the objectives is for the owner to create a self-sustaining practice that can run without his or her presence. While this may work in terms of profitability, it does not serve the clients' best interests.

Although creating a successful legal business model is impressive, its success should come only through transparency and honesty. If one figurehead with a formidable track record of accomplishments is the face of the organization, that person should also be the one overseeing clients' cases. If, instead, the lawyer uses his or her reputation to bring in prospects, never touches the case, and then passes clients to subordinates, this is a form of bait-and-switch.

In criminal law, we're dealing with defendants' lives, their families' lives, and their financial futures. Thus the lawyer upon which your freedom hinges should be the person you signed up to represent your case.

Next, you'll learn about the third level of attorney.

Highest Skill: Expertise and Name Recognition

In Los Angeles criminal defense, a small group of attorneys have been fighting in the trenches, directly representing their clients for years. These industry veterans personally know the cast of characters that I described in the previous chapter. They can identify how aggressive or easy-going a particular prosecutor or judge is and how particular courts run.

Thomas is one of these exceptional lawyers. He is a master of the art and science of criminal defense. First, the science: He's a foremost authority of the law. He also knows courthouse codes of conduct and etiquette and strictly upholds them. He always respects written and unwritten courthouse rules, which is one of the reasons the cast of characters within each courthouse respect him. Next, his years of Los Angeles criminal defense experience mean he's an expert of the ins and outs of each particular courthouse in the countywide system.

For example, when a client has a hearing at 210 West Temple, which is downtown LA's criminal court hub, Thomas knows his client could easily become lost in that court's infamous bureaucracy—every day, it handles Los Angeles's largest and most serious cases. It is charged with coordinating a seemingly endless number of hearings.

Thus, the court maintains very strict rules in order to manage the high volume of cases it handles. Despite what seem like significant obstacles, Thomas has learned to leverage the court's maxed-out caseload to his client's benefit. In fact, on many occasions, Thomas was able to negotiate a better deal in the tough downtown courthouse than he would elsewhere.

In addition, some courthouses have earned reputations among seasoned lawyers. For instance, the San Fernando court is known to be tough on cases related to the sale of narcotics. And the Pomona courthouse is known as a particularly rigid courthouse.

Thomas applies his knowledge of the criminal defense system to his overall strategy. He then addresses the nuances of every case, which represents the *art of criminal defense*. When clients present him with a scenario, he asks himself questions such as:

- Who is involved in the crime in question?

- What is the charge?

- What are the potential ramifications of the charge?

- Who are the prosecutor and judge I'll be dealing with?

- Is the client **sympathetic** or **non-sympathetic?**

What is sympathetic versus non-sympathetic?

Sympathetic clients have had a lapse in judgment but have a high likelihood of making positive course corrections that will lead to better decision making. They often have no prior convictions.

Non-sympathetic clients are charged with serious crimes. They often have a prior criminal record for similar conduct. In addition, the fact pattern of their current case is not one that evokes sympathy. A fact pattern refers to facts about what happened.

Thomas can quickly assess the strengths and weaknesses of a particular case based on years of defending similar cases. And in the courtroom, he quickly adjusts to new information as it unfolds, identifies when and what to negotiate, and can precisely evaluate a prosecutor's position.

For example, Thomas once defended a client in a case in which the prosecutor was eager to move to trial. Prosecutors typically do this for one of the following reasons: They have a strong case they're prepared to pursue, they seek to intimidate the defendant or his attorney or both, or a young, inexperienced prosecutor wants to add a successful case to his résumé as quickly as possible.

Only the best lawyers know how to identify a prosecutor's particular motivation. Meanwhile, mediocre lawyers will frequently misread a situation. As a result, they'll call a bluff when none existed or back off prematurely, which empowers prosecutors.

In Thomas's case, he knew the prosecutor was declaring a premature victory. By aggressively moving the case along, the prosecutor was trying to demonstrate his advantage. Based on the evidence, Thomas decided to call the prosecutor on his bluff.

"Sounds great. Let's move ahead right now," Thomas said, slipping his hands into his figurative courtroom boxing gloves.

The prosecutor didn't expect Thomas to support the decision to move forward. The DA's bumbling backtracking exposed the lack of a thorough investigation and concrete evidence, weak arguments, and a case that, overall, lacked preparation. Now his client had a stronger position, one that would allow Thomas to negotiate more favorable terms on his client's behalf.

The Team Approach versus the Mill Approach

Highest-skill lawyers are typically in high demand. Unfortunately, in a county as large as ours, a sought-after attorney can't attend multiple courts at the same time. In addition, driving from one court to another can be a challenge, if not downright impossible—those of you who have braved the 10 East during rush hour know exactly what I'm talking about. So if you work with an attorney with the highest skill, he or she may still have lawyers on his or her team that take on certain aspects of your case. But this is not the same as the mill-attorney approach.

Whereas the mill approach transfers all aspects of your case to staff attorneys who aren't the firm's advertised figurehead, an attorney at the highest-skill level leverages his or her team to your benefit. Top attorneys are expert managers. They practice at the highest level through working with other trusted attorneys in their practice.

Finding attorneys at the highest-skill level is difficult, mainly because so few of them exist—even in our massive county. Furthermore, identifying this degree of top-notch ability is tough without a clear way to assess a particular lawyer's skill. In the next chapter, I'll provide a checklist that will guide you from the very start of your search, which usually begins online.

CHAPTER 5
Your Online Search

Marco was arrested for drug possession. He worked with a bail bondsman and was released after posting a twenty-five-thousand-dollar bond. Marco's next court appearance was thirty days away. Once he was freed and handed his smartphone, he hopped online to search for a criminal defense attorney.

One website in particular impressed him. The lawyer advertised the high-profile cases he had won over the course of his career, and Marco recalled seeing his face on the side of a bus bench. He hit his phone's call button and requested to speak with the famous lawyer.

The administrative assistant transferred his call to a sales representative. The sales rep then asked him a series of questions about his case, Marco provided answers, and she suggested setting up an appointment.

"Will I be meeting with the lawyer on the website?" he asked.

"You'll be meeting with one of our associates. Be assured that everyone in our firm is fully qualified to meet your needs," she said.

Her answer weakened the initial confidence Marco had felt about the firm. At the same time, he didn't have any way of assessing the quality of a prospective criminal defense lawyer during his initial online search. As a result, he decided to move ahead with the appointment.

In this chapter, you'll learn how to avoid Marco's predicament. I'll help you evaluate the quality of the criminal defense attorneys that appear in your search.

Web Search Pros and Cons

Before the Internet, you couldn't find much about an attorney until you met him or her in person. Unless you had a reliable referral, your resources were phone books, TV commercials, other forms of advertising, and directly contacting the state bar. Even the biggest Yellow Pages ads from the past, however, could never match the amount of content available on today's websites.

Modern mobile devices provide you full access to lawyers across Los Angeles County. But every website is different, which can lead you to experience information overload. A slick and expensive-looking website may draw your attention. But as you learned in the previous chapter, low-skill, middle-skill, and highest-skill attorneys have the same access to online technology. In this sense, the web is a big democracy—both an expert lawyer and a rookie with no experience can build amazing websites.

Thus anyone can promote himself or herself as a top criminal defense attorney. He or she can even make false claims that may remain online unquestioned. With that said, the Internet is a powerful resource to begin your search. Done skillfully, you'll save yourself time by avoiding arranging appointments with attorneys who aren't what they claim to be.

Now, you'll learn how to schedule appointments with Los Angeles's highest-skilled criminal defense attorneys. I'll provide third-party tools that will help you validate claims an attorney makes on his or her site, and you'll learn how to find out if your prospective lawyer has undergone any disciplinary action.

Essential Online Search Questions

1. What is the attorney's area of expertise?

2. How long has he or she been practicing?

3. What is his or her rating on Avvo.com?

4. Has he or she been the subject of disciplinary action?

5. What video content does the lawyer have on his or her site?

Let's explore each of these questions in detail.

1. What is the attorney's area of expertise?

QUESTION: *How many lawyers does it take to change a light bulb?*

ANSWER: *One to change it and two to keep interrupting by shouting "objection!"*

We have well over 1.2 million lawyers in the United States. Which is why lawyer jokes are widespread—attorneys are practically everywhere. But, as I shared previously, common complaints of "this country has too many lawyers" typically refer to the civil arena rather than the criminal justice system. With seemingly endless options when it comes to hiring a lawyer to represent you, finding the highest-skill criminal defense attorney can be a tough task.

You'll find lawyers in Los Angeles who advertise themselves as criminal defense attorneys when prospects are fighting a criminal charge. These same attorneys will claim to be real estate experts when their prospects are looking for help with a property claim. Attorneys like these are likely "Jacks of all trades, masters of none." In other words, they are generalists—lawyers who work in many areas of the civil arena and may, once in a while, take on criminal defense cases or farm the case out to another lawyer and receive a referral fee.

You'll encounter many pitfalls working with a generalist. First of all, if their main focus is the civil arena, they probably rarely defend cases in court. Therefore, by working with a generalist, you're putting your future into the hands of a lawyer who may infrequently litigate cases in front of a judge. In fact, in the civil arena, trials are often discouraged and mediation is encouraged. While civil arena lawyers regularly appear in a courthouse, they're often checking the status of their cases, mediating cases, arguing over evidence or non-responses, filing paperwork, and bickering over inconsequential matters.

Meanwhile, top criminal defense attorneys handle

multiple cases that require them to show up to court nearly every day for arraignments, trials, preliminary hearings, and more. In other words, appearing in front of prosecutors and judges is part of their daily work.

Next, you want to make sure your prospective criminal defense attorney has deep-rooted expertise dealing with your type of case and he or she has local knowledge of your courthouse.

In order to assess your prospective attorney's area of expertise, be as specific as possible in your online search. For instance, if your DUI is in the Van Nuys court, type "DUI Van Nuys lawyer," not just "DUI lawyer." Or if you've been charged with a sex crime and your court is in the San Fernando courthouse, then input "San Fernando sex crime attorney."

When you review the site, make sure the lawyer provides a track record of criminal defense accomplishments associated with the particular court your case is in or the crime you're being charged with or both. Does he or she have a long list of successful cases? In particular, does he or she have information regarding your charge and the court you're dealing with?

2. How long has the lawyer been practicing?

Lawyers will often state this on their site. You want to ask yourself, "Am I confident the attorney has enough experience to represent my interests effectively?"

3. What is his or her rating on Avvo.com?

Avvo.com is a powerful third-party resource to learn about your prospective lawyer. Think of it as Yelp for lawyers with an added layer of objective, unbiased information.

As on Yelp, on Avvo, you'll find reviews. These evaluations from people who have used attorneys are subjective, and reviewers rate lawyers from one to five on criteria, including trustworthiness, responsiveness, knowledge, and "kept me informed." Lawyers receive an overall score from one to five stars.

You'll also find information about the attorney such as practice areas. Here, you can see how much the lawyer focuses on criminal defense. In addition, Avvo provides information about the attorney's fees, payment types, languages spoken, peer endorsements, professional experience, education, awards received, publications, and more.

Lastly, Avvo provides an internally generated rating, which is based on a mathematical model that considers a lawyer's years of experience, disciplinary history, professional achievements, and recognition. This unbiased score ranges from one to ten. Make sure your lawyer has a high Avvo rating: 9.0 to 10.0 is superb, 8.0 to 8.9 is excellent, and 7.0 to 7.9 is very good.

A Word about Online Ratings

You'll find many online lawyer rating sites and directories. Companies with solid reputations operate many of these. Most of these sites originally had a strong merit-based ranking system. In other words, attorneys with the best reputations, reviews, and track records appeared at the top. But because these sites also allow lawyers to pay for top position, regardless of their credentials, it's difficult to tell if the law firm you're viewing is a mill or one run by a highest-skill attorney. In the chapters that follow, you'll learn steps to determine what type of law practice you're contacting.

4. Has he or she been the subject of disciplinary action?
Avvo.com provides information regarding lawyer misconduct, including whether the State Bar of California has disciplined the lawyer. Furthermore, a low Avvo rating is a red flag regarding the lawyer's ability to uphold the highest ethical standards.

The State Bar of California website, www.calbar.ca.gov/, offers another layer of attorney assessment. On the home page, you'll find a search window titled "Attorney Search" where you can input a lawyer's name.

In the search results, you'll find his or her state bar license number and the attorney's current status. If the lawyer has undergone disciplinary action, you'll find detailed information and summaries regarding wrongdoings and the outcome of any action taken against him or her. If the attorney has been disbarred, in other words, is no longer allowed to practice law in California, you can see when and why this took place.

5. What video content does the lawyer have on his or her site?

The highest-skill lawyers are expert orators. During your search, you want to witness evidence of their speaking ability. On his or her home page, make sure the attorney has video content, and then watch it. Remember, this is the professional who will fight for your rights in front of prosecutors and a judge.

Also, the highest-skill attorneys have YouTube pages where they discuss various aspects of the law and describe their expertise. I recommend you visit their YouTube pages and view their clips—particularly ones related to your case.

As you watch their video content, ask yourself the following:

- Is he or she confident and articulate?

- Do the videos reflect a focus on criminal defense, and do they demonstrate local expertise?

- Does the lawyer's delivery indicate the type of professional I'd like to represent me in court?

- Does the lawyer express specific knowledge about the local criminal defense system?

From Online Search to In-person Appointments

Despite the power of the Internet, as a defendant looking for the best lawyer to protect you, an online search is no substitute for a face-to-face meeting. Keep in mind the following:

In most cases, you still must have an in-person appointment with your prospective attorney before you hire him or her.

Your prospective lawyer may be a Los Angeles criminal defense expert, have been practicing for years, have earned a 10.0 Avvo rating, have an unblemished professional record, and have posted a series of impressive YouTube clips. But unless you speak to the lawyer, you'll have a tough time assessing whether that attorney will represent your case or if he or she is the head of a mill practice, which you learned about previously. This is where mill practices are tricky.

The lawyer who appears center stage on a slick, impressive website may be *exactly* the lawyer you're looking for. But once you hire the firm to represent you, your case may be delegated to one of the many lawyers on his or her team, which is okay as long as the top attorney is overseeing the critical aspects of your case.

In this chapter, you've learned how to increase the efficiency of your Internet search. You've learned to separate the highest-skilled attorneys from their low-skilled counterparts. Once you've narrowed your search and compiled a list of attorneys to contact, you may meet one attorney on your list and decide your search is over; you may have performed your research and determined the purpose of your meeting is to confirm your choice; or you may decide to meet with every lawyer on your list before making your final decision. These three options share one common thread: No amount of research can substitute for a face-to-face meeting.

You're now ready for the next step, which is preparing for your appointment. In the next chapter, you'll learn how to make the best use of your time during your initial consultation.

CHAPTER 6
Appointment Preparation

Adrian met with his prospective attorney for the first time. Full of anxiety and fearful of what the future had in store for him, Adrian couldn't wait to tell his account of what happened prior to his arrest to Mario, the criminal defense attorney.

"I was thirsty," Adrian said and continued, "and I really wanted a Slurpee, so I headed to 7-Eleven. It was really hot that day. I was wearing basketball shorts. Later I realized my pocket had a hole in it, which explained why my wallet wasn't with me. But I didn't know I forgot it at the time. And then I got there and went straight to the soda machine to get my cherry orange Slurpee and . . ."

For three minutes, Adrian described the events leading up to his arrest at the convenience store. Mario sat across from him with pen in hand, prepared to note critical information. Despite Adrian's detailed account, Mario's legal pad remained blank—not one word Adrian had said so far seemed relevant to his actual defense. Even if any of the details were important, Mario had no way of knowing this. After another minute had passed, Mario interrupted his potential client and pointed out Adrian's crucial error.

"So Adrian, what's the punchline?" Mario asked.

The defendant raised his eyebrow. His forehead wrinkled. "I'm not sure what you mean," he said.

In this chapter, you'll learn the explanation behind Mario's question. This will help you prepare for your first face-to-face meeting with your prospective lawyer. I'll also provide you a checklist to determine whether the lawyer you're meeting with is the highest skilled and most qualified to protect your freedom.

The Punchline Please

QUESTION: *Why can't a bike stand on its own?*
PUNCHLINE: *It's two tired.*

QUESTION: *I wondered why the baseball was getting bigger.*
PUNCHLINE: *Then it hit me.*

Funny, silly, or absurd, most jokes have a punchline at the end. Without it, a joke would be *a series of nonsensical, disjointed details with no conclusion.* Unfortunately, a defendant's account of events leading up to getting in trouble could also be often described this way.

In regards to criminal defense, a **punchline** is the allegation you're being accused of. It's how the opposing side would describe what took place. The punchline is starting your story with the end in mind. The facts you share will allow the attorney to put the puzzle pieces of your case together in the most precise way. If you lead with this, then as you explain the details, your prospective attorney can understand how events fit together. From there, he or she will begin the process of defending you.

Too often clients will enter their first in-person attorney meeting full of misinformed ideas regarding how to communicate their stories. They've replayed the events leading up to the incident over and over in their heads. They've spoken with friends and family members who not only listened to their description of what happened, but they have also added their suggestions and advice. These well-intentioned but often misinformed people typically begin sentences with, "Here's what you should do . . .," "In my opinion . . .," or "Have you thought of . . .?"

So when the time comes to meet with an attorney, the men and women charged with crimes can't wait to tell their side of the story to a criminal defense attorney. They are eager to add what they perceive are the most important facts, and they begin to spin the case in their favor. Unfortunately, any pre-appointment strategizing and ideas about next steps are usually wrong.

No doubt, a client's account is important. In fact, previously, you learned how a highest-skilled defense attorney will review the police report and compare it to events as you recalled them.

The problem arises when *your* version is full of information irrelevant to your case. Or you attempt to skew the facts in your favor when speaking to an attorney who has not had the benefit of reviewing the relevant police report.

Overall, providing your attorney with an edited version of what happened is doing yourself a disservice. An edited version means you're embellishing your story or you're subtracting facts you don't like in order to make yourself look better.

Always keep in mind, the other side has the unedited facts you've left out, and they'll be ready to use them against you if it serves their objectives. Thus by cutting out crucial information, you're putting your greatest champion—your prospective lawyer—at a disadvantage from the start.

Write It Down

So how do you separate critical details from unnecessary ones, such as the events Adrian described at the beginning of this chapter?

In the past, you've probably sent an email or text message or left a voicemail you wished you could take back. Perhaps you were angry or overly enthusiastic. You stated nonessential and unhelpful information, and you later regretted hitting send or *not* deleting the message. But if you took that same message and just let it sit without anyone else ever reading or hearing it, expressing yourself may have actually helped you feel better about whatever took place. It may have provided clarity in an otherwise confusing situation.

Similarly, before you meet your attorney, I recommend you write down your version of what took place. Describe everything—what led up to the arrest, the incident itself, and what happened afterward. Write about how you felt: Were you treated fairly or unfairly? Were you calm or angry? Imagine you were telling a story to someone who wasn't there. Fill as many pages as you need to do this. Be as detailed as you want.

This exercise will help you share your perspective regarding what occurred. It's the version only you need to see. Maybe you were 100 percent wrongfully accused.

Or perhaps you realize your responsibility, but you also believe you were treated unfairly. Or maybe you regret what happened and are prepared to assume full responsibility. Whatever the case, writing down your account is an important step toward improving the outcome of your first attorney meeting.

Inside the Mind of a Criminal Defense Attorney

In this section, you'll gain insight into the mindset of the highest-skill criminal defense attorneys. This description will point out the punchline's role in regards to a successful first appointment.

Top attorneys have been trained to *begin with the end in mind.* In other words, lawyers' brains are wired to focus on the punchline in order to determine what you're up against. They use the punchline to decide what additional facts are relevant and necessary to strengthen your case.

Remember, top lawyers are hearing stories from a diverse range of defendants every day. Thus no story will shock them. In my case, countless clients have begun meetings with, "You won't believe what happened . . ." and "What I'm going to say will shock you." On rare occasions, prospective clients really do share startling stories with me. But the bottom line is, regardless of what happened, highest-skill attorneys have a set way of evaluating a criminal case, regardless of the fact pattern.

Furthermore, in my experience, the countless stories I've heard are usually similar to other cases I've handled before. And this is how it should be. You want an attorney who has a track record of successfully representing clients just like you. In other words, you want someone who has already been down the legal road you're traveling on—a professional who will be ready and equipped to deal with the eventual problems attendant with your case.

If you reach the punchline as soon as possible, you're more likely to receive the answers you seek and prepare your attorney to defend you properly. Also, your attorney will most likely appreciate your effort to address the essential parts of your case first. This will set your meeting off to a positive start.

In my experience, 90 percent of people who come into my office for an initial consultation know the allegations against them. The allegations may rouse anger and resentment, they may remind the person of how they were mistreated and disrespected, and they may even be scary or embarrassing to talk about. For these reasons, and more, many people are eager to add unnecessary information or delete facts they don't like. But, in terms of forming your best defense, this is not helpful. Unless you're able to state your allegations clearly and honestly, your attorney cannot help you explore your options.

This is why I emphasize jotting your story down *before* you meet with your prospective lawyer. Allow this exercise to describe your point of view. Expressing yourself without placing any restriction on your description will help you complete the next step.

The Punchline Question

Ask yourself the following: *What will law enforcement claim I did in the police report?*

The answer is at the heart of reaching the punchline. You must be able to look outside of your perspective and take on the other side's point of view. In this no-nonsense, direct approach, you imagine you're the prosecutor. Backed by the immense resources of the criminal justice system, what information and evidence will he or she be able to collect and use against you in order to attempt to demonstrate your guilt? This exercise will help your prospective attorney identify the essence of the prosecutor's case against you.

Being objective will be very difficult under your present circumstances. But because most defendants and attorneys will not have access to the police report prior to an initial consultation, attorneys must base their recommendations and advice on your account. (Attorneys typically receive the police report during the first court appearance, which is the arraignment.)

If your story is full of subjective perspectives and unnecessary information, or worse, it leaves out key information, then you cannot expect your lawyer to provide an accurate assessment of your options. On the other hand, if your punchline is solid, you're setting yourself up to receive the peace of mind you seek during this meeting.

In the example you read at the start of the chapter, Adrian *was not* getting to the punchline. He was focused on sharing what was important in his mind, including insignificant information. This prevented him from taking the prosecution's viewpoint. When Mario, his criminal defense attorney, asked, "So Adrian, what's the punchline?" he was urging his client to provide him the information he needed to properly evaluate Adrian's predicament.

Once Adrian understood Mario's question, the allegations against him surfaced. In other words, Adrian gave the punchline, which was as follows.

Starting with the End in Mind

Adrian was accused of robbery with the use of a gun. He was alleged to have taken the weapon out of his pocket, pointed it at the cashier, and stolen the money from the cash register.

Notice how I used "alleged." This reflects language lawyers regularly use. It acknowledges an understanding of the prosecution's side of the story without admitting a client's guilt or innocence. Law enforcement and prosecutors can allege whatever they want. This doesn't mean their allegations will hold up in court when subject to the attack of a skilled criminal defense lawyer.

Whether Adrian actually did what the police claim is irrelevant at this point in the process. (Later on, Mario will address Adrian's guilt or innocence.) What is important is the gun's role in the prosecution's case. It makes any allegation more severe. This critical fact will play a central role in Adrian's defense strategy. Not having this information would undermine Mario's ability to defend his client.

With the punchline stated, the long list of details Adrian shared with Mario at the start of their meeting made more sense: the basketball shorts he was wearing with the hole in his pocket, the wallet that might have fallen out, and the trip to the convenience store to buy a frozen drink.

Family members can also succumb to the pitfall of avoiding the punchline. If a defendant is in custody, then a family member or close friend may meet with the criminal defense attorney instead of the defendant. Rather than stating the punchline, these individuals may give a life story about the defendant. They may make excuses to explain the defendant's behavior. Their intention is typically to protect and defend the person they're describing. But if these friends or family members seek an accurate assessment of their options, they too must state the punchline.

Coming Clean Is Safe and Necessary

Sometimes defendants are concerned what they say to an attorney may put them at risk. They fear stating too much may land them in trouble or cause the attorney to look down upon them. The good news is the *attorney-client privilege* is a cloak that protects you. Everything you say is confidential, even if you never see the attorney again or decide not to hire her.

But if you lie to your attorney or leave out details essential to your case, in the end it will hurt you. It's as if you worked with a top coach to prepare you for the Olympics but never told him you were taking illegal performance-enhancing drugs. Competition day comes, and your coach is ready to be your champion and push you to win gold. Unfortunately, you fail the drug test. As a result, the hard work and preparation between you and your coach are pointless, your coach can do nothing to help you, and you're banned from competing for life.

Unfortunately, throughout my over-twenty-year career as a criminal defense attorney, I've worked with countless clients who have failed to provide crucial pieces of information—essential facts that have later reared up to bite them. Whether during negotiations or in the middle of a trial, I'm always surprised and disappointed when damaging information surfaces I otherwise would have been able to effectively counter if the client had simply told me. As an attorney, my job is to develop a customized strategy for my client's case. The only way to do this is to receive all the relevant information, unfettered by a client's personal spin.

What to Bring to Your Appointment

For defendants who aren't in custody and can therefore meet in an attorney's office, they should bring any paperwork the police provided. If you bailed out, you'll most likely receive a form stating your next court date and the charges against you. You will typically not have the police report.

If a family member is attending the appointment on your behalf, the attorney will ask the following:

- What is (are) the charge(s)?

- What is the bail amount?

- What is the defendant claimed to have done?

- Which court is the case in?

By learning how the highest-skilled attorneys develop their defense strategies on your behalf, you've learned the importance of the punchline. When you arrive at the punchline right away and come clean, you'll increase the likelihood your first appointment will provide the answers you're looking for during this difficult time. The highest-skilled attorneys are able to advocate aggressively on your behalf *only when* they have a clear understanding of the prosecution's point of view and your honest account of what took place.

Now that you've learned how to prepare for your initial consultation, you're ready for the appointment itself. In the next chapter, I'll provide a valuable checklist to guide you through your first meeting.

CHAPTER 7
An In-Person Meeting Is a Must

Jason has been charged with drug possession and is looking for a highly respected Los Angeles criminal defense lawyer to represent him. He reviewed a popular attorney directory website and found a lawyer with the credentials he is looking for. Tiffany received the highest ranking on the website, which motivated him to research her further.

On her website, Tiffany stated she had a career spanning eighteen years and had performed over one hundred jury trials. She also had a series of videos where she described her expertise dealing with drug charges.

Jason made an appointment to meet with Tiffany. He arrived at her impressive office located in a high-rise. An administrative assistant escorted Jason to the conference room. Shortly after, an attorney met with him. But it wasn't the woman he saw on the website. The lawyer introduced himself to Jason.

"I'm Robert, and I'll be representing you," he said.

Shaking Robert's hand, Jason sat down and asked himself, "What happened to Tiffany?"

In this chapter, you'll learn why Jason's appointment with Robert could put his personal freedom at risk. If you've followed the checklist I previously provided, you've narrowed your list down from hundreds of prospective attorneys to one or two. Now, you'll determine both whether the criminal defense attorney you're meeting is the highest-skill lawyer and how to avoid an attorney bait-and-switch.

Your Attorney Interview Checklist

1. Am I meeting the lead attorney?

2. What punishment am I looking at?

3. How well-rounded is the attorney?

4. What's the attorney's likeability?

5. Will the lead attorney go to court?

6. Is the attorney well-known locally and respected in the courthouse, and does he or she know the prosecutors and judges?

Once the attorney answers these questions, you'll have a feel for whether you're meeting with the right person. Here is what you should look for in those answers.

1. Am I meeting the lead attorney?

Previously, you learned the importance of working with the highest-skill lawyers. The Essential Online Search Questions have helped you narrow your search to the lawyers who have the credentials, experience, and track record to defend your case in the best possible way.

But no matter how much prior research you perform, unless you meet the lawyer in person and ask directly about his or her role in your case, you'll have no assurance the attorney you're considering hiring will be the same professional representing you in court. Thus when you set up the initial consultation, ask if you're meeting the attorney you're interested in hiring. If the answer is no, most likely this is a mill practice.

As you recall, mill practices have big marketing budgets, which they use to pay for TV, print, and online advertising. They rely on the reputation of a successful figurehead to bring in the high volume of clients necessary to cover their massive advertising budgets and overhead.

Mill Practice Bait-and-Switch

Imagine you've gone through the Essential Online Search Questions and have scheduled an appointment to meet with a particular lawyer. In other words, you've taken *the bait.*

Now, when you arrive at the office, you wind up meeting with a sales representative or another attorney in the firm. You discover the attorney that motivated you to set the appointment in the first place isn't in the office. In other words, the highest-skill attorney has been *switched* with someone else.

The bait-and-switch business model is the one the mill practices often follow.

The scheme they've established is as follows: They've built a business based on the credentials of one prominent attorney. He or she is the figurehead and may have created an online profile that appears on a well-respected lawyer directory highlighting his or her accomplishments. But what the profile doesn't disclose is the figurehead no longer appears in court representing clients. He or she may not even show up at the office—and may not have done so *for years!* Rather, the mill practice has a team of inferior attorneys who will represent the high volume of clients entering its doors.

No doubt, some defendants are completely content working under such an arrangement. But if you're looking for the highest-skill attorneys, the mill practice model will come up short. After all, when you're in the courtroom, what will prosecutors think about the credibility of the firm representing your case when its figurehead doesn't even practice anymore?

Although Los Angeles is one of the largest cities in the country, the criminal defense community is small. Highest-skill attorneys see each other in courthouses, and they follow one another's careers. In my case, because I'm in court nearly every day and have been for over two decades, I know the figureheads for most mill practices haven't appeared in court in years.

Only attorneys who are in court on a daily basis are able to determine what you should and shouldn't do regarding your case. Their hands-on approach ensures your case is negotiated or tried properly.

To make matters even more challenging for consumers looking for the highest-skill defense lawyers, even the most well-respected and popular online directories—ones that boast about their objective ratings and time-tested ratings formulas—promote mill practices. For example, you may see the headshot of a lawyer attached to a practice. He or she may appear at the top of a search.

"This number-one position must mean this lawyer's the best," you tell yourself.

Sometimes a number-one position signals the attorney has earned the top spot. Other times the impressive search result may be less about solid credentials and more about paying top dollar for high online placement. Sometimes both reasons are the case. Thus, a top position could have various meanings about the lawyer—highest skill, mediocre, a mill lawyer, paid for top placement, no longer appears in court, appears in court every day, or various combinations of the preceding. What a confusing mess! The simple solution? A face-to-face meeting with your prospective attorney.

2. What punishment am I looking at?

Once a highest-skill attorney has a complete story regarding your case, he or she will be able to identify your options and next steps, describe what is feasible under present circumstances, and educate you on the law in regards to your particular circumstances.

In addition, when you're at risk of losing your freedom, you'll probably want to know what the best- and worst-case scenarios are. A solid defense lawyer, who has years of experience defending clients like you, will base his or her evaluation on your answers to the following questions:

- What was your behavior in the crime?

- What's your criminal record?

- In which courthouse is your next hearing set?

Let's explore the last question. The highest-skill criminal defense lawyers have represented clients in courthouses throughout Los Angeles. Thus, they understand the nuances of the particular location. They also know the judges, the prosecutors, and the other members of the cast of professional characters you learned about previously. They'll leverage their knowledge of the courthouse to develop their overall strategy.

3. How well-rounded is the attorney?

Imagine a potential lawyer says the following on his or her website:

> *I'm a former prosecutor, so I know the system
> you're dealing with better than anyone else!*

I've read some version of this description on various criminal defense attorney advertisements. You may have seen similar ads in the tax industry: "I used to work for the IRS, so I'm here to help you during a tax problem."

In the case of former prosecutors, their background as city or district attorneys isn't necessarily a big advantage over a criminal defense attorney who has never been a city attorney or DA. In particular, you should consider the ratio between years as a prosecutor and years as a criminal defense lawyer. The number of years as a criminal defense attorney has more significance. Thus, you should give it more credibility.

For instance, Stan may have served as a prosecutor for fifteen years. But he's been a criminal defense lawyer for only five. Meanwhile, Jennifer has never worked as a prosecutor, but she's been a top Los Angeles criminal defense lawyer for over twenty years. In regards to this checklist item, Jennifer, in my opinion, is more qualified.

This is because prosecutors have the full backing of the judicial system. They have the legal weight and massive government budgets supporting their efforts. Meanwhile, criminal defense attorneys are charged with representing their clients knowing the legal weight and massive government budgets are working *against* their clients. This trains the highest-skilled attorneys to develop winning strategies, despite the inherent imbalance between both sides. In summary, you want a criminal defense attorney with twenty years of experience defending people like you and not one with twenty years of experience only prosecuting them. There's unmatched expertise that comes from an attorney who has been preserving and protecting people's rights and freedom for over twenty years versus someone who has been taking it away and making sure people go to jail.

Former prosecutors may also be ex-city and ex-district attorneys for a reason. Although they are promoting this experience as a benefit, they could have been fired or the subject of a lawsuit. If part of their advertising hinges on connections and special relationships with prosecutors, then a bad reputation within the courts may hurt your case.

The Complete Package Attorney

Next, a well-rounded criminal defense attorney knows when a case should be negotiated or litigated. He or she has the experience to do either. Thus, it's not a matter of personal preference, not a case, for instance, of an attorney steering his or her client to negotiate because the lawyer is more comfortable negotiating rather than litigating. The highest-skill attorneys are equally capable of doing both, so their advice to you is based on what approach will best serve your interests—not on their comfort-level regarding their abilities.

Ask your lawyer, "How many cases have you litigated?" and "Do you have a preference between negotiation and litigation?"

Negotiation versus Litigation

Negotiation is when you take the position, "I accept I committed a crime." From this point, you do damage control in order to experience the best possible outcome based on your particular circumstances. Or sometimes, depending on the circumstances, a skilled defense attorney does damage to the prosecution's case in order to have a stronger negotiation position.

Litigation is when you try your case in front of a jury or attack the prosecutor's case by way of motions designed to upend his or her case prior to trial. Perhaps this is because you refuse to accept the prosecutor's offer or because you are downright innocent.

Based on the evidence, the prosecution can't always tell if the defendant is in a position to negotiate or litigate. Under most circumstances, the prosecution assumes the defendant is guilty.

In addition, prosecutors know the attorneys who mostly negotiate. These lawyers typically avoid litigation and may not feel comfortable defending a case before a judge and jury. If the prosecutor realizes this, it may put the defendant at a disadvantage.

4.   What's the attorney's likeability?

After you meet with your lawyer, ask yourself the following question:

Do I like this person?

If the answer is yes, then judges, prosecutors, court staff, and other professionals probably do as well. In other words, if your prospective attorney can sell you on his or her abilities and you feel comfortable with him or her, that same lawyer can sell and be liked by the cast of professional characters as well.

This is yet another reason why a face-to-face appointment is essential. You can answer the likeability question only if you meet the lawyer in person.

A lawyer's likeability will benefit your case in countless tangible and intangible ways. Criminal defense has many ambiguous areas. For instance, many rules and procedures are either flexible or have room for negotiation. You need an attorney who can leverage the goodwill and political capital he or she has earned through years of practice and relationship building within the criminal justice system to navigate through the nuances of your case.

5. Will the lead attorney go to court?

As you've learned, the highest-skill attorneys are actively practicing law and representing defendants in court every day. In order to fulfill this particular checklist item, ask the following three sub-questions:

a. How often are you in court?

The prospective lawyer may not attend every single court appearance related to your case. But if he or she goes to court every day, which is what all successful LA criminal defense attorneys do, then the lawyer has fulfilled this requirement. And this means when push comes to shove, your attorney will be there for you.

b. How involved will you be with my case?

The attorney you're considering hiring must be the leader of your case. With that said, the highest-skill attorneys often have support staff, including lawyers, working in their firms. A good leader knows how to delegate and make himself or herself available for the heavy-lifting aspects of your case.

In other words, it's okay if the attorney you hire doesn't make every court appearance—this doesn't necessarily make him or her part of a mill practice.

It's *not acceptable,* however, if the lawyer no longer makes any court appearances at all.

c. Who will oversee investigations and motions?

In conjunction with his or her research attorney, the lead attorney should be strategizing the investigation of your case utilizing the law and motion work, if applicable.

Whichever attorney you choose, the best will figure out a strategy to address most effectively your issues. He or she will set your case up and oversee its successful outcome. The highest-skill attorneys will use motions and investigations to leverage the case in your favor.

When it's time to execute the most critical parts of your case, you want to know your lawyer will be by your side. For example, during your preliminary hearing, your champion must be there for you as your strongest ally. After all, you want someone who can challenge the prosecution when the need arises.

In particular, the highest-skill lawyer's responsibilities include arguing motions, negotiating with the judge and prosecutors, and conducting preliminary hearings and litigating trials. In order to fulfill their unflagging commitment to their clients, these attorneys have created a client-service model that includes a well-trained support staff.

Los Angeles County covers nearly 503 square miles. One highest-skill attorney cannot appear in multiple courtrooms at the same time. The best attorneys directly handle all critical aspects of your case, oversee trusted attorneys that work with them as they perform routine tasks, and frequently use other attorneys to make meaningless court appearances. This team model is different from a mill practice. It is a more effective way to represent clients because it allows the head attorney to delegate non-essential tasks to attorneys and staff, which frees him or her to focus on the most important court appearances— ones where his or her skill will benefit you most.

The bottom line is the lead attorney must be the person overseeing your case, supervising directly, making final decisions, and communicating with the prosecutor and judge when push comes to shove. Allow me to illustrate.

Kristen is bailed out, and her arraignment has been set. Scott, the highest-skill attorney Kristen hired, may have one of his attorneys file any necessary paperwork and handle the straightforward court appearances that are easy for a properly trained lawyer to take care of. Next, upon researching Kristen's case, Scott may believe the police conducted an illegal search.

As a result, Scott will then have his team attorney draft the motion for Scott's review. In addition to drafting motions, this attorney often conducts research on behalf of Scott's clients, communicates with clients when Scott is not available, and may make some court appearances. Throughout the process, Scott is directly overseeing his clients' cases. At the same time, he is using his limited time to focus on the most critical aspects of a particular case.

Some cases need investigation and time before they are seasoned to the point that Scott's participation is necessary. Thus, leveraging his team members to manage his time is perfectly acceptable and effective. It allows Scott to travel from courthouse to courthouse, negotiating and litigating cases ripe to be dealt with.

Think of Scott as a closer. In pro baseball, an ace pitcher (or closer) is often warming up in the bullpen throughout a game and preparing to make his appearance on the mound when his team needs him most. When it's time for him to show up, he's ready to bring his team to victory.

The highest-skill attorneys are master closers. They have established an efficient client service model, which includes delegating non-essential tasks. This allows them to do what they do best: negotiate or litigate the best possible outcome for their clients

In a mill practice, a closer, like Scott, doesn't exist. Kristen's case would immediately be handed to a staff attorney. This person may be fresh out of law school or have only a couple of years of career experience. He'll review the case, determine the issues he'll argue, and then write motions to support his position. Although the steps he'll go through may be similar to those of a highest-skill attorney, he lacks insight developed over years of battling cases, the track record of success, the familiarity with the local courts, the connections among the cast of professional players, and the negotiation and litigation skills that come from years of representing a wide range of clients. The mill attorney won't have the *it* factor that makes the lead attorney the best person to close your case.

Think of it this way. If you were to place your bets on a boxing match, would you wager your hard-earned cash on a fighter who just learned to box or the athlete who has amassed a string of victories and continues to stay in top shape?

6. Is the attorney well-known locally and respected in the courthouse, and does he or she know the prosecutors and judges?

Previously, you learned about the cast of professional characters: judges, prosecutors, bailiffs, and court staff. Your attorney will be interacting with many people. Maintaining clear communication and earning the respect of the cast of professional characters will provide you immeasurable benefit. This relates to the previous point I made about the ambiguous and nuanced aspects of many cases. Having solid relationships with the cast of professional characters could mean the difference between a mediocre outcome and one that exceeds your expectations.

Also, lawyers who know a judge's judicial temperament and the prosecution's tendencies in a particular courtroom will use this information to develop your strategy. For example, prosecutors run the range between rigid and open-minded.

Rigid means prosecutors' sympathies favor the victim far more than the defendant. They pay little or no attention to the defendant's circumstances, and they seek the harshest punishment possible for any given crime, no matter what.

Open-minded means prosecutors maintain compassion for the victim. At the same time, they realize the defendant has his or her perspective as well. Rather than focus on the harshest punishment possible, they consider what punishment has the highest likelihood of setting the defendant up for a successful crime-free future.

Keep in mind these are two endpoints within a range. A prosecutor may fall anywhere between rigid and open-minded. With that said, in my experience in courtrooms throughout Los Angeles, most prosecutors lean toward the rigid end of the spectrum. Lawyers who know a particular courthouse's prosecutor, judge, and the court staff will develop a strategy based on this priceless insider knowledge.

Your Criminal Defense Attorney Is Your Champion

Think about if you were on the operating table having your appendix removed. This is a routine procedure that takes place every day in hospitals across the country. In the vast majority of cases, your surgeon could perform the procedure successfully without giving it much thought. But what if you reacted adversely to the anesthetic and you suddenly went into cardiac arrest? At this point, your surgeon taps into his greatest ability and training. He is responsible to successfully navigate your body out of life-threatening danger and toward a safe recovery.

Criminal defense attorneys play a similar role in your case. Every case is different. Some are more complicated than others. Thus, not all of them will require an attorney to tap into his or her greatest skills. But when you're dealing with a prosecution with immense resources at its disposal, you want to make sure your attorney has the skills to steer your case through multiple what-if scenarios and guide you from the beginning to the end of your criminal case.

The focus of the next chapter is negotiation. You'll learn how the highest-skilled attorneys use their years of experience to advocate on your behalf. Through their track records of success—built on decades working in the Los Angeles County criminal justice system—you'll set yourself up to experience the best possible outcome.

CHAPTER 8
Negotiation

It was Tuesday morning, and several attorneys were waiting to speak with the prosecutor in charge of their clients' cases. This is a common practice in courthouses across LA County. As each attorney presented his or her best arguments to the prosecutor, it was evident some clearly knew what they were doing while others had no clue.

Over the course of my twenty-plus-year career, I've waited my turn to speak with prosecutors countless times. It provides me a first-hand opportunity to witness how my criminal defense colleagues work. I'm always amazed at some of the unskillful approaches I see. And I'm sometimes shocked at how little some lawyers know about the criminal justice system.

That Tuesday, I presented my case to the prosecutor. During our negotiations, he and I had reached a mutually respectful impasse. As a result, I calmly asked for a **chambers conference**, and my request was quickly granted.

What is a chambers conference?

This is a private meeting between the judge, the prosecutor, and a criminal defense attorney that takes place in the judge's chambers. Defendants aren't allowed to attend these.

While I waited for the judge to permit my chambers conference, I was able to watch my colleagues deliver their cases to the prosecutor.

SCENARIO 1
Sara Skillfully Negotiates on Her Client's Behalf

Sara, a criminal defense lawyer with a solid reputation, presented after me. She provided bulletproof arguments, skillfully advocated on her client's behalf, and as I had seen in the past, adjusted her communication style to match the prosecutor's temperament and tendencies. Had her client been permitted to attend this meeting, he would have been thrilled with Sara's professionalism and expertise.

But despite her stellar efforts, Sara hit a roadblock. The prosecutor was known in lawyer circles for treating criminal defense attorneys with disdain. He ignored her arguments and wouldn't budge.

If he could, he would have told Sara to take her arguments and pound sand. While a lesser attorney would have given up, Sara was a sophisticated lawyer with a pit-bull-like tenacity. She looked the prosecutor in the eye.

"I completely understand your position. In the interest of doing everything I can to help my client and advocate on his behalf, I'm sure you won't mind if I request a chambers conference with the judge," she said.

Sara stated her position politely and respectfully. And just as I had done before her, Sara then walked to the clerk of the court and requested a chambers conference. The judge granted Sara's request.

Sara made a power move with implications only a local, savvy attorney could pull off.

First, many judges in Los Angeles county will not meet with defense attorneys in chambers. They are reluctant to take actions that may challenge the prosecution's position. But Sara knew the judge overseeing her client's case. Judge Alvarez had a reputation of being fair and open-minded. He was unfazed about disagreeing with prosecutors. In addition, Sara had a solid argument on behalf of her client.

SCENARIO 2
Jack, the Amateur, Burns Bridges

The next attorney to make his pitch to the prosecutor that morning was Jack. The LA criminal defense community is small, and I didn't recognize him. Perhaps he was a new attorney. Or maybe he was a generalist, someone hired by a client who didn't know the importance of working with a lawyer whose practice focuses on criminal defense and is local to the courthouse. Whatever Jack's background, his inexperience was clear.

The prosecutor expressed frustration with Jack's arguments. Jack, in turn, became more defensive and criticized the prosecutor's judgment—it was a personal attack that resulted in even more hostility between them.

The prosecutor was angry and unyielding, and Jack knew they wouldn't come to an agreement. Like Sara and me, Jack also asked to have a chambers conference with the judge—it was as if he saw what Sara and I had done and simply copied our strategy. Judge Alvarez accepted.

The Chambers Conference: Sara, Jack, and Me

Once Judge Alvarez was ready for the chambers conference, Sara, Jack, the prosecutor, and I went to meet the judge.

My case was discussed last, which gave me an opportunity to observe Sara and Jack present their arguments.

Sara met with Judge Alvarez and the prosecutor first. The judge was receptive to her reasonably and eloquently stated arguments. As a result, her case swiftly and successfully wrapped up. She exited the chambers standing tall and ready to share her good news with her client.

Based on what I had witnessed earlier, I knew Jack was ill-prepared and didn't know how to adjust his delivery to match his audience's temperament. Meanwhile, all highest-skilled attorneys knew Judge Alvarez was fair but a stickler for protocol. His decisions typically reflected a hands-off approach, unless the argument was very solid.

When it was his turn to speak with the judge, Jack complained about the prosecutor's **offer**.

What is an offer?

It spells out the terms of a proposed agreement to settle a case between the prosecution and defense.

This ruffled the prosecutor's feathers and strengthened his resolve to maintain his position and undermine Jack's. The prosecutor subsequently verbally lashed out at Jack during the chambers conference.

"I have no idea why you requested this meeting in the first place. A complete waste of everyone's time!" the prosecutor said.

The inexperienced lawyer was dumbstruck. Nervous and clearly shaken by the prosecutor's venom, he bumbled through the rest of the conference, unable to argue effectively on his client's behalf.

In a cringe-worthy display, Jack's argument centered on the prosecutor's unreasonableness versus the merits of his client's case. The judge swiftly declared Jack's complaints and arguments as groundless.

I wished I could have pulled the rookie lawyer aside and told him, "You just can't make personal attacks. Like it or not, prosecutors and judges are often friends. They're in court together all the time. For all we know, Judge Alvarez attends barbeques at the prosecutor's house. By your attacking the prosecutor, Judge Alvarez won't work with you to resolve your case."

Unfortunately, Jack's client suffered the consequences of his lawyer's incompetence.

Jack's chambers conference request horribly backfired. Negotiation was no longer an option, the DA was mad, and the case was set to go to trial, which was a bad strategy for Jack's client. To make matters worse, Jack's client had no idea about his lawyer's botched move and the bad position he was now in.

The opposite was true for Sara's client. By politely and professionally resolving the case by court intervention, Sara did not burn any future bridges with this particular prosecutor. At the same time, she employed all opportunities available to her client. This is just a small example between strategies of the best attorneys and those of attorneys that shouldn't be practicing criminal defense.

The Trial Is Often the Only Option

When you read the words "criminal justice system," what comes to mind? Images of courtroom jury trials were probably high on your list. While depictions of jury trials appear on TV shows every day, the truth is only a small percentage of cases actually go to trial. In fact, the criminal justice system, with its limited courtrooms and ever tightening budgets, isn't equipped for every case to go to trial. Therefore, prosecutors usually won't file a case unless they have solid evidence against someone.

So what is the most common route cases follow? The overwhelming majority are resolved through negotiation. Only those small numbers of cases that cannot be negotiated result in a jury trial.

You'll rarely see depictions of negotiations in popular media. Thus the focus of this chapter is to provide essential insight into what this process involves. You'll learn what negotiation is and how the highest-skilled attorneys use it to their clients' advantage.

What Is Negotiation?

In the criminal defense world, negotiation is supposed to be a series of discussions between your attorney and the prosecutor, your attorney and the judge, or your attorney, the prosecutor, and judge with an eye toward resolving your case with the most favorable terms possible.

In order for you to experience the best result, your criminal defense attorney must be a master negotiator, in other words, someone with extensive local expertise and who has been immersed in the LA criminal justice scene for years. Your face-to-face meeting, which you learned about previously, will usually give you a solid idea whether you're dealing with a savvy veteran or someone unseasoned.

Buyer Beware: Outrageous Claims by Mill Practices

Previously, you learned about mill practices. Typically, one prominent figurehead attorney represents the face of the practice. This figurehead created a successful criminal defense track record but no longer shows up in court defending clients. In fact, many years have passed since the figurehead even regularly showed up at the office. In his or place, this lawyer employs a team of lesser-experienced attorneys.

Mill practices often make questionable claims in their advertising. Unsuspecting callers may be connected with a salesperson who assures them, "We'll be able to get your case dismissed" without knowing details about your predicament. Making such claims is irresponsible and dishonest. Even the callers themselves often realize what they're hearing is too good to be true.

I know of one mill practice that specifically targets those who have been charged with a DUI. In her ads, the attorney argues you should *never* plead guilty. For someone unfamiliar with the criminal justice system and panicking over his DUI charge, not pleading guilty seems like a great idea. The underlying message is of freedom, having charges dropped, and a clean record.

What these unsuspecting men and women don't realize is the vast majority of those charged with DUIs plead guilty to some type of offense. This decision to plead guilty usually leads to the best outcome, given the adverse circumstances. Sure, a person charged with a DUI may decide to plead not guilty and have his case go to trial. But he'll probably lose both his case and the ten thousand dollars or so he paid the unscrupulous lawyer, someone who made promises that could never be fulfilled. Meanwhile, the lawyer continues to earn big bucks through advertising that gives the appearance she can win every case.

Thankfully, knowledge is power if it is used properly. Because you're reading this chapter, you won't fall prey to misleading mill practice advertising tactics.

How the System Works

When you think of Los Angeles County's criminal justice system, compare it to the branches of the United States government. The president, in the executive branch, is commander-in-chief. The United States Congress, in the legislative branch, is charged with managing domestic affairs.

Similarly, judges have the most power when it comes to issuing punishments, which are also called sentences. Meanwhile, prosecutors hold the authority to charge someone with a crime.

At some point in the process of defending the charges against you, your attorney will meet face-to-face with one or several decision makers. These include the judge, a head district attorney, or any number of prosecutors.

This meeting can take place under various circumstances. It can occur during an Early Disposition Program (EDP), which you learned about earlier. In this instance, the judge, prosecutor, or both have reviewed your case, and they're prepared to discuss it, which could lead to a resolution.

Overall, you won't encounter a set method for the negotiation process. Each courthouse and even individual courtrooms within a specific courthouse follow their own procedures. Also, each case is different. In other words, there are no one-size-fits-all formulas. This is why experiencing the best possible outcome requires working with the highest skilled attorneys. They know the nuances of each courthouse, they understand the specifics of your case, and they develop their strategy according to their experience and connections.

The Art of Negotiation

In order to create the best result for you, the highest skilled lawyer knows exactly how to navigate the many people and bureaucratic hurdles that could prevent a favorable deal.

In regards to people, the highest-skilled attorney has created a solid reputation among judges, prosecutors, and law enforcement. In other words, the attorney knows and understands how to address his or her audience. Over the years, I've witnessed less seasoned attorneys make inappropriate, irrelevant, and even offensive comments in the courtroom. Because many key negotiation aspects take place in the courtroom, such poor judgment can forever damage the credibility of the attorney in question and the client's case.

Judges: Judicial Temperament

The criminal defense attorney's knowledge of a particular judge's judicial temperament is important to the lawyer's overall negotiation strategy.

For instance, imagine an attorney and DA have reached an impasse. Under certain circumstances, as discussed earlier, the lawyer may decide to reach out to the judge to resolve the matter. Perhaps, he or she requests a chamber's conference. This is how Jack, Sara, and I met with Judge Alvarez in the story I shared at the beginning of the chapter.

Judges have total discretion over this request. Not all judges want to involve themselves in the negotiation. They may be concerned with appearing as **undercutting** the prosecution. Thus when making appeals to judges, timing and prior experience with the judge are key. The highest-skilled attorney knows which judges to approach and when the judge will be the most receptive.

What is undercutting?

This is a judge's decision to decrease the punishment reflected in the prosecution's offer.

Once in chambers, attorneys must know how to adjust their argument style. This is different from what occurs in a large courtroom *on the record,* which means a court reporter is taking down everything stated and a lawyer can request an official transcript for a fee.

Prosecutors: Rank and Location Matter

As you learned previously, prosecutors include deputy city attorneys and deputy district attorneys. Among prosecutors, a hierarchy exists. At the top are the Los Angeles County district attorney and city attorney. Everyone else is a deputy. When you think about the size of our county, you can imagine what a huge responsibility these people have.

Take the LA County District Attorney's Office for example. It is the largest of its kind in the nation. It supervises about one thousand deputy DAs, nearly three hundred investigators, and about eight hundred support staff. Los Angeles County citizens elect the LA County district attorney every four years. He or she has an appointed administrative staff similar to the cabinet of the president of the United States.

District attorneys are ranked from one through five where five is the top grade a DA can attain. Ranking is based on a series of tough civil service exams, time on the job, and promotions by the head DA, administration, or both. Attorneys who are ranked grades one and two often work in the arraignment courts. Grades four and five lawyers frequently staff trial courts.

While the hierarchies are strictly maintained, a particular DA's grade isn't necessarily public information. Thus attorneys have no way to explicitly identify a DA's ranking. The highest-skilled attorneys, however, know the grades of many DAs through word of mouth, countless courtroom appearances, and meetings with members of the cast of professional characters you read about previously.

The grading system is one of the many pieces of information a highest-skilled attorney uses to develop his or her client's overall negotiation strategy. For example, imagine a grade-four DA writes an offer inside a DA file related to a particular case. It will indicate what the prosecutor wants the defendant to plead guilty to and what the proposed punishment will be.

Using the above example, let's say a grade-one DA presents the offer to the defense attorney at the EDP. Without knowing the grade of the presenting DA, an inexperienced attorney may dispute the offer's merits and argue changes be made.

Meanwhile, a highest-skilled attorney knows when a grade-four DA writes an offer, a grade-one or grade-two prosecutor doesn't have the authority to change it. Thus arguments presented to the grade-one or grade-two DA are a waste of time. Instead, the negotiation will have to take place with the grade-four DA, another grade-four DA, or his supervisor.

Next, the Los Angeles County District Attorney's Office also assigns and reassigns DAs to courthouses throughout Los Angeles. DAs don't stay in the same courthouse their entire career. For instance, a DA may have worked in one juvenile court for years. A highest-skilled lawyer may have crossed paths with this DA many times. Suddenly, the DA may be assigned to a new courthouse. This kind of movement takes place regularly, and the highest-skilled attorneys use this to their advantage whenever possible. For instance, the next time that particular DA handles a case against the lawyer's client, the defense lawyer will try to leverage her knowledge of the DA's tendencies to her client's advantage.

Working with Prosecutors: The Devil Is in the Details

The long-term relationship between DAs and highest-skilled attorneys means they know the most effective way to communicate with a particular DA, regardless of his or her current courthouse assignment.

In addition, each DA has his or her own prosecution style. Some are rigid. If you present rigid DAs a proposed resolution, they'll usually reject it right away without thoughtful consideration.

I have dealt with some high-positioned DAs who abhorred meeting with criminal defense attorneys. They don't necessarily dislike defense lawyers; they simply don't want to be bothered with meetings. Scheduling an appointment with them will spell disaster for your client's case. Thus, for lawyers, it is always in their client's best interest to steer clear of setting up a meeting with these particular DAs. Instead, they would be better served leveraging other negotiation tactics with a different DA or the judge.

If a prosecutor is being unreasonable, a lawyer may decide to reach out to the prosecutor's supervisor. This is only advisable on an as-needed basis. You have to know when to do this and under what circumstances. Sometimes I've used this approach when dealing with a case where the prosecutor made countless mistakes, which reflected he was a beginner, incompetent, or both.

In instances of serious and sophisticated crimes, an attorney may set up an appointment with a head DA, who has ultimate responsibility for that case. Once the head DA presents his or her final offer, the defense attorney will have a tough time negotiating a better future deal on behalf of his or her client. As a result, highest-skilled attorneys focus on these high-stakes meetings above others. They will require the attorney to leverage his or her greatest skill. Meanwhile, the lead defense attorney will assign non-critical appearances and tasks to his or her team members.

An attorney's reputation is on the line when negotiating with DAs. He or she never wants to be perceived as being sneaky or underhanded. So whatever tactic a criminal defense lawyer uses must uphold the reputation he or she has built or chooses to portray. The lawyer must always respect judges, prosecutors, and the process while zealously defending his or her clients.

Courthouse Locations Influence a Lawyer's Strategy

Previously, you learned about rigid versus open-minded prosecutors. These descriptions apply to courthouses as well. A courthouse's culture often reflects the community it serves. Where a courthouse falls in the rigid versus open-minded continuum helps a criminal defense attorney develop his or her strategy.

Some courthouses have a reputation of being rigid, which means the prosecutors and judges often seek the maximum punishment possible. The courthouses in the cities of Pomona and West Covina have this reputation. Other courthouses are known to be less harsh. The downtown Los Angeles courthouse—where a large portion of Los Angeles County criminal cases are heard—is known to be this way. Jury selection in downtown Los Angeles courts offers criminal defense attorneys a wide selection pool, which frequently benefits a client's case. Overall, in my opinion, Van Nuys and the San Fernando Valley courts fall in-between rigid and open-minded.

The Role You Play in Negotiation

Previously, you learned about the punchline. I shared the importance of taking on the prosecutor's role when explaining the events that led up to the charges against you. I also described how being upfront and honest about your role in the charges in question is essential to developing the best possible strategy. Being honest is not necessarily just about admitting guilt or innocence; it also involves providing your lawyer with the facts necessary to counter any of the prosecution's allegations.

If you did commit the crime you're charged with, your lawyer will need to know the *why* behind your actions. Also, reveal any details that will assure the judge and prosecution you've learned your lesson and vow never to let this particular behavior occur again. In many instances, your criminal defense attorney will use this information during negotiations.

When I meet with head DAs and my client admits guilt for a crime, the DA often asks, "Why did your client commit the crime?"

If I'm able to provide a sensible response based on my client's account, the DA understands what led my client to commit the crime, and the client can demonstrate his or her pledge never to repeat the malfeasance again, my client has a better chance of receiving a lesser punishment than would otherwise be the case. If, on the other hand, the DA is convinced my client will not stop committing crimes, he or she is much more likely to punish my client as harshly as possible.

When the Deal Is Unacceptable to You
I've had clients tell me, "I know I did something wrong. But I'm not guilty of what I'm being charged with."

As a result, the client refuses to accept the charges against him or her. If the client is ready to forego negotiation and litigate—in other words, undergo a jury trial—I'm ready. I'm confident my courtroom skills will provide my client the best possible outcome.

If the charges are inappropriate, I may be able to have them reduced to reflect the actual crime committed. In which case, the crime may be less serious than the one alleged by the prosecution. Or maybe all charges will be dropped outright.

Whatever strategy I develop is not an assurance my client will have all or any charges dropped. It means that whatever the result, it is the best one he or she will have experienced based on his or her particular case. And I base my ability on my successful track record representing similar cases.

All highest-skilled attorneys are equally confident as I am in negotiating and litigating cases. They know how to assess a case to determine which strategy will work best. Sometimes assuming a defensive posture is the most effective. For instance, if the client is, without a doubt, guilty, then the attorney is doing his or her best to negotiate a less severe punishment.

Other times, developing an offensive strategy is in the client's best interest. If the client is clearly innocent, the highest-skilled attorney will file motions, obtain evidence through investigation, and dismantle the prosecution's case, piece by piece.

If the case is close—in other words, it is too difficult to determine what the client's outcome will likely be—a highest-skilled attorney knows how to present his or her position in a way that doesn't reveal the client will accept a deal no matter what. This is because once prosecutors know an attorney won't fight his or her client's charges, the lawyer has lost leverage.

Negotiation Represents an Attorney's Highest Skill

Many times, lawyers will informally bounce ideas off their colleagues in and around the courthouse in order to gain insight from respected perspectives. They do this while always upholding attorney-client privilege. For example, walking in and out of the courthouse, a lawyer will bump into a colleague. Or more likely, he or she is sitting next to an attorney in the courtroom waiting for the judge to come out. Sometimes even when the judge is on the bench, law-yers can whisper to one another. On occasion, inexperi-enced attorneys will ask me basic questions that call their credibility into question. They'll inquire about simple paperwork, such as a courthouse form any experienced criminal defense attorney would have seen countless times before.

"I'm not sure what to do with this," the inexperienced lawyer will tell me.

His confused expression makes it clear the attorney is asking me for help.

After steering the lawyer in the right direction, I wonder how his clients would feel if they knew their lawyer didn't know what he was doing.

They paid good money to this attorney—perhaps they were lured in by a mill practice's slick advertisement. Little did these clients know their attorney was learning on their dime. Clearly, highly effective marketing does not a solid, seasoned attorney make.

Becoming a lawyer is hard work. To earn the title juris doctor (JD) and to pass the bar require discipline and hours of work. But what you learn in law school and need to know to pass the bar prepare you little for negotiation in the real world of the Los Angeles criminal justice system.

No doubt, to negotiate effectively, an attorney must have a mastery of the law. But that's just the beginning. Negotiation also requires an ability to communicate effectively to unrelated individuals and groups: clients and their families, law enforcement, courtroom staff, prosecutors, and judges. Only a lawyer who can skillfully communicate with all parties in a case can effectively advocate on his or her client's behalf.

In addition, a master negotiator knows the culture of each particular courthouse and even each courtroom within a courthouse, identifies when to take an offensive or defensive position, and leverages his or her reputation to benefit a client's case.

This chapter has pointed out to you the countless variables that influence a case. Only through years of dedicating one's career to Los Angeles criminal justice does a lawyer have the knowledge and experience required to represent his or her clients in one of the nation's largest and most complicated criminal court systems.

In my experience, a client is best served by an attorney who possesses both street smarts and book smarts. But this is just the start. Your champion must know the system through years of litigating cases in it and understand the political landscape where your case is being heard. Your lawyer must be well-respected and local to the court in order to achieve the best result possible, whether through artful negotiation or sophisticated litigation.

CHAPTER 9
Always Seek Local Expertise

At the beginning of my career, I took on every case I could get my hands on. I had a voracious appetite to learn as much as possible about LA's criminal justice system. I strongly believe if we pour ourselves into what we love *and* improve the lives of those around us, our ability to reach goals and set higher ones is limitless.

I love what I do every day because it gives me the opportunity to improve lives and decrease fear and suffering. In particular, being able to help men and women to follow a better path and get them on track again is one of the most fulfilling aspects of being a criminal defense lawyer.

Also, being a Los Angeles County native, I know firsthand we live in one of the most diverse, regulated, and developed regions in the world. And our criminal justice system matches the size, scale, and complexity of this massive metropolis. Ever since I embarked on my law career nearly twenty-five years ago, I've embraced the challenge of mastering LA's criminal justice system consisting of law enforcement, prosecutors, lawyers, and nearly forty courthouses.

I've enjoyed amassing the skills that have made me one of Los Angeles County's top criminal defense attorneys. The reputation I've earned in and out of the courtroom over the past two decades allows me to represent my clients in a way only a handful of Los Angeles criminal defense attorneys can.

Considering how big our county is and the amount of cases that run through the court system every day, you'd be amazed at how small the criminal defense community is—the most experienced professionals know all the key players and can quickly separate the pros from the rookies and amateurs.

No doubt, navigating our state and federal criminal justice system is both an art and science. All top-performing attorneys are masters of the law and courts and appreciate the role of the most important individuals in our justice system. They are also skilled negotiators, expert orators, and compassionate advocates.

Sometimes the best approach is to negotiate a plea bargain while other times, if negotiations fail or if the client is innocent, the defense attorney must be able to try the case in front of a court or jury and win. The highest-skill lawyers use their extensive experience to choose the customized strategy that will bring the best results for their clients.

My clients count on me to leverage the countless hours I've spent in courthouses throughout LA County, in front of judges, and negotiating with prosecutors. Los Angeles is home to many of the nation's most high-profile criminal cases, and I've been directly involved with many of them. From courtroom drama that has made front-page news to cases you'll never hear about, I'm proud of my track record of accomplishments and helping my clients regain their peace of mind, overcome one of the greatest obstacles they'll ever face, and have a chance to do the right thing.

I'm a firm believer in the US justice system. No doubt, it has its weaknesses—decades of experience have given me an intimate understanding of its shortcomings. Nevertheless, I'm convinced our nation has one of the world's best criminal justice frameworks. And it's one that is dynamic and continually evolving. This is both a strength and a challenge—it constantly adapts to change, but unless lawyers stay active within the system, rather than sitting on the sidelines or infrequently representing criminal defense clients, their skills will quickly become obsolete. Which explains why my sole focus is Los Angeles criminal defense. When my client's freedom is on the line, I'd better be a specialist and know the local scene better than anyone else—*and I do.*

Within these chapters, you have gained the tools to find the best possible lawyer to advocate aggressively on your behalf. While no lawyer, no matter how talented and hard-working, can guarantee a particular outcome, the advice, checklists, and recommendations in this book will guide you on your path to developing the perfect defense.

About the Author

Ronald D. Hedding, Esq. is the founding member of Hedding Law Firm, which consistently ranks as one of Los Angeles County's top criminal defense law offices. For over twenty years, Ron's career has focused on criminal defense in Los Angeles. He has been lead counsel in some of LA's most high-profile criminal cases. From *CNN* to the *Los Angeles Times,* Ron regularly provides legal commentary to the media and has been profiled in prominent print and online publications. When he's not defending clients, Ron is committed to serving his community. Over the past ten years, he has coached over forty youth sports teams. He is a native of Los Angeles and is the proud father of four children.

To Learn More about
The Art of Criminal Defense
and Criminal Defense in Los Angeles

Visit Ron Hedding's website at
HeddingLawFirm.com
or phone 866-986-2092.

You can also purchase *The Art of the* PERFECT DEFENSE
at your favorite online stores such as Amazon,
Barnes & Noble, Google Play, and iTunes.

Scan here to learn more: